MW01205837

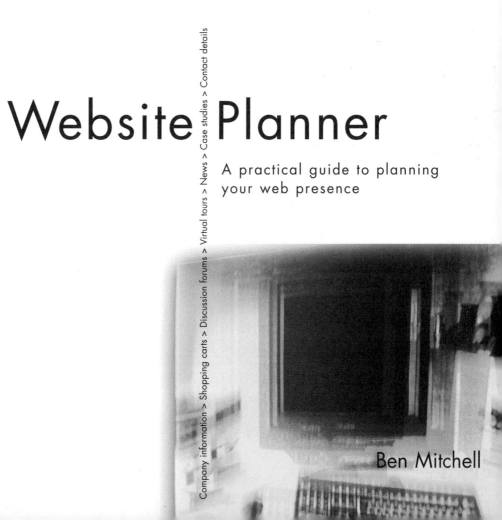

Website Planner

Company information > Shopping carts > Discussion forums > Virtual tours > News > Case studies > Contact details

A practical guide to planning
your web presence

Ben Mitchell

Website Planner

Company information > Shopping carts > Discussion forums > Virtual tours > News > Case studies > Contact details

A practical guide to planning
your web presence

Ben Mitchell

Pearson Education Australia
Unit 4, Level 2
14 Aquatic Drive
Frenchs Forest NSW 2086

www.pearsoned.com.au

Commissioning Editor: Mark Stafford
Managing Editor: Susan Lewis
Cover and internal design by Belinda Street
Typeset by Midland Typesetters, Maryborough, Vic.

Printed in Australia by Ligare

1 2 3 4 5 06 05 04 03 02

National Library of Australia
Cataloguing-in-Publication Data

Mitchell, Ben, 1960- .

   Website planner : a practical guide to planning your web presence.

   Includes index.
   ISBN 1 74009 715 7.

   1. Web site development. 2. Web sites - Design. I. Title.

   005.72

An imprint of Pearson Education Australia.

Contents

Chapter 9—What are you going to put on the website? 55

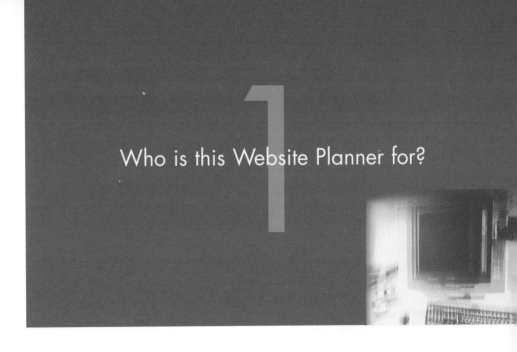

Who is this Website Planner for?

This book is for anyone involved in the planning of a website, whether for a commercial, government or not-for-profit enterprise. This workbook focuses on defining the why and what of website development—why build the website and what to build. There is plenty written about the 'how', so for now we will leave that to the web designers and technical people.

Who should complete the Website Planner?

Small businesses

For some businesspeople, website development is a DIY project. Small business owners are likely to understand the commercial realities of their companies and be able to complete the workbook on their own. To complete the planner effectively you will need to know (or find out) the answers to the following questions:

> Who are your prospects?

> Who are your customers?

> What is so special about your company?

> What do prospects want to know about your company?

> What would help your existing clients to do business with you?

> How do you want the world to perceive your company?

This workbook calls for information with a marketing and business focus. It also requires input relating to the operational and fiscal realities of the business.

> Where does the profit come from?

> Which clients or prospects do you focus on?

Large businesses

In the majority of cases, IT managers, website managers and other staff cannot complete the workbook without the input of others within the business. For these people, the Website Planner provides an excellent framework with which they can develop a sound business case for the website.

A successful website requires input from those in management who understand the organisation's communication and marketing processes, its clients, and the costs of doing business.

Executives need to understand the role of technology in their businesses and in their industries. These days it is very rare to find a CEO who does not have a good grasp of the value of the systems that drive their businesses. What CEO can turn a blind eye to the investment required to develop ERP and other large-scale operational systems?

> ERP (Enterprise Resource Planning) is a broad term which covers activities that enable managers to manage facets of their businesses. These facets include inventory, product planning, financials, purchasing, human resources and much more. For more details go to www.whatis.com. ▶

A technology industry, including some of the world's largest software companies, is riding on the back of ERP. Many of the biggest IT projects occur in the ERP space. All ERP systems are more or less capable of communication over the Internet too, which means that soon the systems and companies will look after themselves, and we will all be sitting on an island somewhere sipping cocktails. (How's that for a vision?)

There are some CEOs who still don't use computers. Not too long ago I heard of one who gets his secretary to print out any emails he receives and he dictates the replies, which are to be mailed so he can sign them. People like this are an oddity.

Managers need to take control of all facets of their business, including what they do on the Internet.

Why I developed this workbook

In my work as a Business Development Manager and consultant in the web industry, I have spent hours speaking with businesspeople about what they are doing or planning to do on the Internet. These people are often managers working in senior positions within organisations. These organisations range from large publicly listed conglomerates, to small- and medium-sized enterprises. Without exception, these businesses recognise the need to address the Internet in some way, shape or form. Many of these businesses have spent large sums of money getting their businesses onto the Internet already. (Sometimes 'large' is a relative term; sometimes 'large' is very big bucks!)

The biggest challenge businesses seem to have is working out what they want to do on the Internet. So much has been written and talked about, so much money spent and wasted, that many of us are scratching our heads and asking what we should do next. It has become an exercise in clear thinking.

> What should we put on our website?

> What do we tell the web developers we want?

> How do we make sure we don't do the wrong thing?

This is where I come in and start asking some of the questions I ask in this Website Planner. Before long the erstwhile confused businessperson puffs out their chest, looks me in the eye, and says, 'go away and I'll send you a brief that I want you to quote on'. In other words the penny has dropped and they have taken control of the situation.

I want to give businesspeople a logical framework with which they can take control of what their company is doing on the Internet. Specifically, I want to help businesspeople develop a rationale for their company website.

Benefits of the Website Planner

The benefits of using this workbook to develop your website plan include:

> You will reduce the risk of wasting money on a website that does not suit your business.

> You will develop a solid business case for your company website.

> You will have the opportunity to revisit some of the fundamental values that define your company.

> You will address the issues that drive your website project in a logical fashion.

> You will be in a position to give clear direction to web consultants, and ensure that what they provide meets your defined business needs.

> You will be able to use the workbook as grounds for productive communications within your company.

> You will focus on the factors that shape your business.

> You will develop an increased awareness of your customers' needs.

> You will save money and time.

The process of identifying what the website should do and why, can take big businesses months and thousands of dollars to work out. Smaller businesses go through the same pain.

Those in smaller businesses often get to the stage of throwing their hands up and getting the web designer to recommend and start building something—anything. Or they may try to adapt (or copy) another business site, saying 'Let's see what the bloke up the road's got on his website and take it from there.'

This workbook is your fast track to understanding how you can effectively use your website, and what it should include.

There are hundreds of books on all facets of the Internet. Like many of you, I have spent time in bookshops trawling through the titles. If you are keen, you can read a few books and start to form ideas about what you might have on your business website. In my opinion this is the longhand way of doing it. It is also approaching the issue from the wrong end.

> This workbook is for people who don't have the time to read fat and largely irrelevant texts on the subject, but know they want to get their website working effectively for their business.

> This workbook will steer you through the process of deciding what you should have on your website and why.

Intranets versus Extranets

This workbook will focus on business websites only. More specifically, it will focus on websites that are aimed externally at the World Wide Web, as opposed to Intranets, which are websites aimed internally at staff. Having said that, I will refer to the value of having secure information on websites, accessible only via password access. The secure areas work like Intranets except that they do not sit on your company's own local network; they are on the Internet. These secure areas are often called Extranets. They are just sections on websites that require login via password and username. For the purposes of this book I will refer to them as 'secure areas'.

2

The story so far

Dot-coms

Some months ago I was sitting in my office, busily discussing an issue with a colleague, when in came our CEO, crowing about the fact that 'we' had acquired another Internet company and our stock was climbing 'out of sight'. That same day I went to ask a question of another senior manager of the same company. He was intently examining the rise and fall of our share price on his laptop. There was talk that so-and-so had bought himself a new sports car, and that so-and-so was being interviewed by a current affairs program that evening.

Was this the new economy? Things were certainly new, I'll say that. People were in jobs where they really had no idea what they were doing (I saw it first hand). The blind were leading the blind! The system was in overdrive, and the most popular mottoes were 'give it a go' and 'he who hesitates is lost'. From a new economy point of view, if you weren't doing business on the Internet, you were soon going to be out of business.

I was working in what was known as a 'dot-com'. Dot-coms were those companies that were seen to be driving the Internet movement. These companies were seen to be part of the 'new economy', and were regarded as 'sure bets' by the investor community.

It was around this time when one of my old friends, a financial analyst with a particularly sceptical attitude towards 'new' anythings (and rightly so), appeared on television talking about a changing of paradigms. He had been forced to acknowledge that the world was hell-bent on making the Internet into the primary platform for global commerce, almost overnight. This is the guy the blue chips look to for even bluer-chip advice! Make no mistake; there was virtually no way anyone could resist the new economy movement.

The investor community treated traditional companies that confessed to having no strategy for e-business very harshly. I know there were some conservatives who could smell rats, but for most of us it was move with the crowd or get trampled.

What happened then? The companies that had no real business model did not deliver (of course). Dot-coms with wildly overblown expectations came crashing down to earth, the sources of their capital pulling out as they fell. As a result, the stock prices of so many tech companies, good and bad, crashed to new lows. 'Visionary' CEOs who once could do no wrong were asked to 'move on' by their boards. Millions of investment dollars from both the institutional investors and the mums and dads were lost in the rush for the door.

What did these companies say in their business plans about revenue streams and cash flow? The world thought it was matter of 'build it and they will come'. The faster we get online, the faster we will all be multi-millionaires. Yeah, right.

> I guess it was a bit like the word getting around that a particular horse is a 'sure-fire thing'. It didn't matter that the horse had attention deficit disorder, the bookies could barely cope with the rush. The odds fell and the rumour mill worked overtime.

When the race started the horse wandered out of the gates and watched the other horses gallop into the distance. The pundits were telling each other not to worry because when ▶

the horse did go, it would go like a rocket. They even managed to con the bookies into taking extra bets after the race had begun. The bubble burst after the other horses had been washed down, fed and watered, and had gone to bed for the evening. The pundits stood there watching until some lousy kid yelled at them that the horse was never any good to start with.

In the next minute hundreds of people charged the remaining bookies and stole their money back. Those who had previously made their money on the horses decided that all horses were bad, and some of them went and reclaimed feed from the stables.

Amidst all the shouting and crying it was discovered that the trainers who had started the false rumours about the horse had become rich and invested their money in biotech companies.

Now we wait and watch for the survivors as they scramble from the ruins. It will be these survivors who will shape the Internet from here on. Cynical boards of directors from traditional businesses will demand to see sound business plans before companies are allowed to move a muscle in any way related to the Internet. Consumer behaviour will slowly right itself and we will probably start using the Internet in ways we have not thought of yet. (Someone will be thinking of these new ways, don't worry about that.)

Media on the Internet

Recently I attended a discussion regarding the future of traditional media and the Internet. In attendance were a number of highly respected members of the media community, as well as people with considerable experience with this new economy of ours. It was agreed that we still haven't worked out viable business models to support much of what is happening on the Internet.

Do the principle distributors of news and information ask consumers to subscribe to their services, to gain access to a more personalised or niche delivery of information? Is advertising going to continue to support media as it has done in the past with print, television and radio?

> Newspaper sales have been steadily decreasing ever since the Internet started pumping information free of charge to its expanding audience. Newspapers are finding it harder and harder to make a profit. As the readers of the news on the Internet increase, it means reduced sales of newspapers, and therefore reduced income from newspaper advertising. My tip is that before long the major titles will be charging a fee to access their content online. This at least will pay for their infrastructure as a media distribution organisation. As far as the actual newspapers are concerned, there will continue to be consumers who prefer the format of the newspaper to that of the page on the Internet. Will these numbers be sufficient to sustain the costly production of the newspapers themselves? I doubt it.

The past has clouded the popular perception of the Internet. To say that it has been a failed experiment is wrong. Despite everything that has happened, more and more people have been choosing to use the Internet to find all sorts of information. The Internet has not delivered the riches promised, but people are coming in droves to see what it is offering.

Some statistics

According to the Australian Bureau of Statistics, over one-third of Australian households have Internet access. Almost 800,000 of these households went online in 2000. Over 482,000 Australian businesses are connected to the Internet. (These figures were released in June 2001.)

> **B2B**

That's 'business to business' in case you haven't heard of it already. Please note that there is also B2C (business to consumer), G2C (government to consumer), B2E (business to employee), E2E (employee to employee). There is also Me2C, which is what I plan to do for my summer holidays (that's 'me to sea'—get it?).

Above and beyond businesses using the Internet as a marketing and communications medium, there has been considerable investment in using the Internet to streamline and automate B2B transactions. This new phenomenon will allow businesses to automatically generate purchase orders and have them sent to their suppliers. In turn, the suppliers' systems will manage the sales process, with the goods requisition process kicked off, and the billing process completing the transaction without human intervention (in theory).

Promoting your business via your website

Despite the hot and cold history of the Internet, there is a greater acceptance of the medium than ever before. We may not be trading online at the (unrealistically) high rates that have been forecast, but we are still using the Internet as a vital medium for business communications.

Ask yourself, where do I go to find out about a company or service these days? I know that many of you will have answered 'the Internet'.

I firmly believe that the majority of businesses should have a good website to support them. If your business offers a range of products or services, and has a good story to tell, you'd better tell it on the Internet if you want it to be heard.

Of course, many businesses will decide not to use the Internet at all. Some small businesses like medical practices and local accounting practices may decide not to worry about having their own website. I would encourage them not to forget about registering with the Yellow Pages however. Never before have the Yellow and White Pages and other online business directories been so accessible—local businesses can now be located quickly using postcode searches.

Traditionally we have used directories like the White and Yellow Pages to find businesses of particular types. Now, more and more of us are using search engines to find the companies we are after. What does this mean for the directories? Will there be a point when it is no longer worth paying a premium to have your half-page advertisement in the Yellow Pages? What will happen to the phone books if their revenue source is significantly diminished?

Conducting business via the Internet

Currently, many millions of dollars are invested in different software, all seeking to become the 'standard inter-business transaction platform'. The universal challenge is to develop a generic platform standard for communications, which will allow a company to transact online with any or all of its suppliers and customers. My system and your system need to speak the same language if they are going to work together. Microsoft is in there with most of the big business software players. Although it is accepted that common standards are required, the financial imperative will inevitably push the big players into developing their own proprietary languages, in order to grab and 'lock in' a lion's share of the pie.

Suffice to say the mess will take some time to sort out.

The scope of this integration of companies' systems is still taking shape. The degree to which Internet and related technologies will shape the way companies do business is still to be determined.

So you already have a website

Many businesses in Australia and around the globe already have a website. Some businesses may have multiple websites, and others may be up to the third or fourth version of their website.

I heard it said recently that the majority of companies that do not have a web presence now don't need one. This is probably pretty close to the truth for large organisations. There are, however, a lot of smaller organisations that have yet to broach the issue of a website. Some businesses have held off to see what happens with the Internet; others have not had the resources to put into such a project.

The process of developing a second- or third-generation website should be much the same as coming up with your first website. The major difference is that you have experiences from which you can learn. Each subsequent website should be an improvement on those that have gone before. Many questions that need to be answered with regard to your new website can be answered by reviewing your existing website.

What's wrong with the existing website?

There are a number of issues that I have seen arise when companies that have an existing website are developing a new website. Let's look at some of them here.

Don't like the design

If it looks cheap it probably was. Getting the website to reflect your company brand is a design issue and is best left to skilled graphic designers. Would you approach your company based on what you see on the website?

The content is out of date

Which content is out of date? Does some of the content change regularly or frequently? If so, there are ways to manage this. Do you have people who can keep the content up to date? Was there a breakdown in communications between your business or marketing staff and the webmaster or IT?

Don't know if anyone used it

Did some people say the website was good, and others a waste of time? Did your webmaster or hosting provider give you information on how many people were looking at your website and which parts they were looking at?

> **Hint:**
>
> *If the hosting provider told you the website was receiving thousands of hits every day, and you are not a major source of community information or entertainment, what were they talking about? Why would thousands of people come crashing through your front door every day? Why didn't those same people contact you en masse to ask you about your business? Could it be that this figure was not all it seemed?*
>
> *[For more information on measuring website traffic, refer to the section Traffic Measurement on page 29.]*

Management don't know it exists, and don't care

Does the website sit anywhere in your company's marketing or business plan? Has it always been treated as something special which has its own rules? (Remember that that's what they said about the new economy. Remember also that they were wrong.)

Danger!

Many businesses both large and small have invested inordinately large sums of money creating their websites, only to find that they have not delivered the riches promised. Not only that, many of the companies who have spent big bucks on their first website actually hate what they have. Think carefully before you decide that you will never again bother about the Internet. Remember that thousands of companies worldwide share your frustration. The problem you face is the false start that we all had. The Internet is now being used like never before. Prospects and clients are doing their research on the Internet; can you afford not to be there?

Review your existing website

This section contains some questions for you to answer with regard to your existing website. By answering these questions you will prepare yourself to tackle your new website.

First, here is an example of how one business (a not-for-profit charity organisation) might answer them.

1> *What were the main objectives you were trying to achieve with this website? To what degree do you think you achieved each of these things?*

> *to get potential customers to contact us*
> *to provide information to current customers*
> *to reduce the amount of phone calls received for information*
> *to improve our level of customer support*

> we tried to get potential clients to contact us. We asked people how they found us and 13 people said they found us through our website.

2>   How does the existing website portray your business?

> It makes the business look tired/small/new/interesting/dynamic/boring/technical/complicated/slow/friendly/cheap/weak.

3>   What does it portray well?

> brand—colours, logo, general style
> technology—diagrams, look and feel, case studies are good.

4>   What does it portray badly and why?

> Not-for-profit focus—styling too corporate, looks like technology company, focus on money, pictures of holiday locations are out of place.

5>   Did you get feedback on this website? What was it? Who gave it to you?

> Five visitors to the website mentioned typos on the site.

> Two major sponsors rang; they both said the site made us look like a high-tech company in the dot-com fast lane.

> A manager from our UK branch said the site did not reflect our organisation's position because it did not try to portray a community style; there were no pictures of the people we are trying to help on the major pages.

> Lots of people said that our map approach to the case studies was really good.

6>   Who was/were your target market/s? Are things they are likely to want on the website? Are they easy to find?

> The website was originally built for anyone looking for our organisation, especially potential donors.

> They were likely to want to know what campaigns we were running and how to donate.

> The information was OK but we made them contact us using an email form which no one ever answered.

> *The phone number was on the website but it was only in the corporate sponsorship section and hard to find.*

7> Is the content of the website up to date?

> *Most of the content does not really change except for a newsletter.*

> *The newsletter was only published on line twice so it was a year out of date.*

8> If not, why not?

> *We really didn't have anyone with the time to write the newsletters, and then when they were written it was a nightmare getting the CEO to sign them off because she is always travelling overseas.*

> *Our web company closed down so we had no one to make the changes.*

9> What do you like about your website?

> *The descriptions of the campaigns we ran and the rollover navigation headings on the home page.*

10> What do think could be improved?

> *Make the design look less techy and more down to earth.*

> *Make the contacts for each user group more obvious.*

> *Have pictures of the people we look after throughout the website.*

> *Use white as the background colours on all of the pages, as the multi-colours are too loud and confusing.*

> *Make the website look a bit like our new marketing brochures.*

> *Get rid of the links pages, and the game page, as they don't do anything for our organisation.*

11> Are there any other points worth noting about your existing website?

> *The drill-down maps we used to present the case studies were really good. Everyone liked them.*

12> *What would you do differently as a result of your first website experience?*

> Make sure the design of the website had something to do with our organisation.

> Make it easier for people to contact us by phone, fax or mail.

> Put in links only to our sister sites not dozens of sites like we had.

> Put some educational content in there for schools to work with.

> Use a larger web design company.

> Get a content management system built in so we can make changes to content when we want.

> Don't involve the CEO in the process of changing content unless necessary.

> Put a secure area on the site for staff to look at where we can put important internal notices.

> Use the logo of the organisation properly. It was lost in multi-colours.

Use these questions to develop opinions about your existing website. Write down the answers in bullet form. Get as many thoughts as you can out of your head. You can refer to your answers later as you plan your new website.

1> *What were the three main objectives you were trying to achieve with this website? To what degree do you think you achieved each of these things? If you were trying to attract new business, did you get any because of your website?*

_____

_____

_____

_____

_____

_____

_____

_____

_____

2>   How does the existing website portray your business?

_____

_____

_____

3>   What does it portray well?

_____

_____

_____

4>   What does it portray badly and why?

_____

_____

_____

**5>   Did you get feedback on this website? What was it?
Who gave it to you?**

_____

_____

_____

_____

_____

_____

6> *Who was/were your target market/s? Are things they are likely to want on the website? Are they easy to find?*

_____

_____

_____

_____

_____

_____

7> *Is the content of the website up to date?*

_____

_____

8> *If not, why not?*

_____

_____

_____

_____

_____

_____

9> What do you like about your website?

_____

_____

_____

_____

_____

_____

10> What do think could be improved?

_____

_____

_____

_____

_____

_____

_____

_____

_____

**11> Are there any other points worth noting about your
existing website?**

_____

_____

_____

_____

_____

_____

12> *What would you do differently as a result of your first*
website experience?

_____

_____

_____

_____

_____

_____

_____

_____

_____

_____

Large multi-segment websites

Some universities and large companies have websites that are very large
and unwieldy. In the case of companies that have grown by acquisition,
and universities that have many different faculties, these websites are
often made up of many smaller websites, each with a different look and
feel, and different content architecture. Over time these organically grown
websites become more and more difficult for their target audiences to
navigate. Due to their size and complexity, the content usually goes out
of date.

If you are in this position, you will face some or all of the following issues:

> Some of the businesses or departments involved will not want to consider any sort of consolidation of the website. They want to have total control over what they do.

> Arriving at decisions in terms of global branding will have to involve input from the various stakeholders. Managing this input will take considerable political savvy and care.

> There may be numerous different web servers (computers) pushing content into the total website. These require maintaining and, at times, upgrading.

> The different areas of the business may have signed contracts with numerous hosting providers. Some of these contracts may incur penalties if they are not honoured.

> The architecture of the content may reflect the organisational structure, not only of the organisation as a whole, but also of the various departments within the greater organisation. Users of the website may find it difficult or impossible to locate content and achieve what they want to do.

> The determination of a solution that can globally manage the entire infrastructure is clouded by the fact that every vendor says that their solution can do everything for you. Sorting the wheat from the chaff is an exercise that could take months in itself.

My advice—unless you are experienced with large IT projects, get help. Why?

1> You need an expert and a devil's advocate who can bring an impartial view to the table. (The various stakeholders are likely to be comfortable that they are getting an equal say in the outcome if there is someone slightly removed in the driver's seat.)

2> By choosing an external web provider, you will garner expertise in the areas of usability, graphic design and website infrastructure technologies, and the resources to affect change where it is required. (Unless there is a stated and pressing business impera-tive that the website be rationalised, you will find it hard to secure internal resources as you require them.)

3> An independent third party familiar with the technical solutions available will be able to make an objective assessment of viable alternatives, without pitching you much of the marketing fluff. (If the process of platform selection is done externally by a truly independent party, you will have less chance of your senior management being sold a solution that does not meet your explicit requirements. There are many examples where companies have been sold a bus where a bicycle would have been more appropriate.)

4> As the project driver you will be able to see the woods for the trees, if you are not directly burdened with the task of delivery. You want to be in a position to manage stakeholder expectations of the project. Politics can drive a project or disable it; therefore it has to be managed.

The successful website

Goal setting

I think success can be explained as the achievement of goals. Sometimes we can stumble onto success; it still means we have still achieved something that we are happy with or wanted to do.

For the purposes of your website, it is difficult to measure the success of a website if there is no yardstick by which success can be measured.

Why was the website developed in the first place?

> To generate hits?

> To generate new customers?

> To keep your current customers happy and spending money?

Every website needs to have some criteria against which it can be measured. A manufacturing company might develop a website to reduce the amount of requests they receive for educational materials from students and schools. In this instance, the reduction in phone calls and time spent preparing and distributing materials for students and schools could measure success.

As you read and work through the Website Planner, you will identify the goals by which your website should be measured.

Your business plan

Once upon a time a company's web strategy was seen as somehow divorced from the company's business plan. It even took a while for companies to accept that what they were doing online should be considered part of the marketing plan. The truth is that your online activities should be an integral part of your overall marketing and communications. As such, they should be treated with as much care and deliberation as any other part of your business. In fact, for many businesses the web has become their most effective means of promoting their business to the outside world. These businesses need to make sure they are sending the right messages. It's one thing to wear ties in the office, but if your company looks like a backyard operation on the Internet, then that is how the viewers of your website will know it.

As you complete the Website Planner you will address many of the issues involved in the business planning process. The end product of this workbook could form part of your business or marketing plan. Some of the thinking you will do will surely supplement what you have (or haven't) done for your business plan.

> ## Metadata
>
> What is 'metadata', I hear you say? Good question. If you go to an established website like amazon.com and press the right button on your mouse, you will bring up a menu that contains 'View Source'. View the source.
>
> Providing the source code is visible, you will be able to scroll down and see a clump of words called metadata. In the case of Amazon you should see:
>
> <meta name = 'keywords' content='amazon. com, amazon books, amazon, amazon.com
>
> ▶

books, amazon music, amazon.com music, amazon video, amazon.com video, auctions, amazon auctions, amazon.com auctions, electronics, consumer electronics, gifts, amazon gifts, amazon.com gifts, cards, e-cards, e-mail cards, greeting cards, amazon cards, amazon.com cards, toys, amazon toys, amazon.com toys, games, amazon games, amazon.com games, toys & games, toys and games'>

This is the stuff that search engines use to classify your website in their databases. To learn more about how these search engines work, go to www.whatis.com and see what you can find under 'search engines' and 'crawlers'. The search engines basically take what is written in your website meta-data as a fair representation of what is on your website.

If I were a scoundrel and trying to attract many eyes to my website, so I could unscrupulously claim revenue from unsuspecting advertisers (a practice that is dying a natural death), I might include terms such as 'basketball' and 'scantily-clad ladies' in the metadata. People will only be annoyed that I have misled them when they get to my website and find information on 'Hub caps in the former Soviet Union'. Annoy the wrong people and you are liable to find out how damaging hackers and viruses can be. (Yes, people can hurt you via your website!)

Similarly, I'd be a fool not to include the terms that are relevant to my business so that my target audience can find me.

Bringing people to your website

Ask yourself, when you want to find a website the address of which you don't know, how do you find it? If you answered that you would use a search engine then you are like the vast majority of the online population. Search engines are the street directory and phone book of the web rolled into one. In short, if your website is not being displayed by the major search engines then people are not going to find you. Don't listen to anyone who says otherwise. Don't expect that people will remember your web address, no matter how catchy it might be (unless you are as big as Yahoo or Amazon, and even then these guys are well registered—check them).

Here are my recommendations in a nutshell:

> Make sure your website's metadata contains all of the keywords and phrases people might use when they are searching for your site. Talk to your web provider about this.

> Register your website with the popular search engines. Currently, I would recommend Excite, LookSmart, AltaVista and of course Yahoo. In reality there are dozens of search engines available. If a particular search engine seems to service the industry you are in then by all means register with it. Registration with Yahoo involves parting with some money; my inclination is that the money is well spent if yours is a serious business. If on the other hand your website is more of a hobby there is probably no need to use their subscription-based section. Yahoo uses the normal robot-type search engine 'Google' as well as the subscription-based area. The difference will be performance for users who are not overly familiar with Yahoo and search engines in general.

> Check periodically how the major search engines perform at calling up your website when you enter the name of your company, and some of the keywords and phrases associated with your business. If your website doesn't appear, get your web provider to make sure it does. (Expect to pay for a few hours work as this may take some fiddling.)

Compare how your website performs on search engines relative to those of your competition. If your competitors are out-performing you, try to have a look at the source code on their websites to see what they have put in their metadata.

Traffic measurement

I have lost count of the times that people have said to me that their websites get 'hit' umpteen thousand times a week.

There has been plenty written in the media about the different companies and software that measure website traffic. What I will say is:

> Is the number of hits relevant to your business? Think about it. Unless your business is utilising an advertiser-pays model, how can you generate money from people walking through your 'store'? Keep this in mind.

> The only way to get a good feel for the use of your website is by looking first at 'user sessions'. Forget 'hits' and 'pages down-loaded'. There is too much ambiguity surrounding these terms.

> If you are a small business in a niche industry, and your Internet Service Provider (ISP) is telling you that your website is receiving 10,000 user sessions daily, have a good think why. Is there mis-leading information in your search metadata? Is yours a business dealing in pornography, sport, entertainment or an equally popular field?

> Get the ISP to show you the reports they are generating for your website. If they are unable to do so, either get a copy of your web-site logs from your ISP, and have these run through web-traffic measurement software (your web provider should be able to help you organise this) or get a new ISP.

Here are some things you should be able to learn from the reports:

Where your visitors come from

The report will tell you what people are entering into search engines. You can adjust your metadata accordingly.

The number of people who visited your website

Was it 10,000 per day or 200 per month?

The times of day your website was visited

If your website has a lot of traffic, and you want to provide a high level of service, at what times can you afford to have downtime? Do you have to fork out for 24x7 service at 99.9% availability? In other words, should you pay for the top level of service from your hosting provider or ISP?

The content that was viewed and how often

Learn what your visitors are looking at when they get to your website. Are your clients accessing the information you provided for them? Have you told them that it's there? Is it worth spending money on upgrading the catalogue to an automated system if no one is using the current manual one? If the visitors are prospects, what are they looking at? Is it presented in a fashion most conducive to winning their business? Should you expand on the content they are looking at to make it more effective?

Go through the reports with your web provider. Have a good think about the results from a business perspective. Use the traffic reports to understand user behaviours and use those behaviours to manage your website. If you think visitors should be accessing particular content and they are not, move it to a prominent position on the website. Because you understand your business, you may well discover ways to improve what you are offering on your website, and in your business in general.

If the website does not seem to be working, change it.

Sticky websites

Once upon a time (last year), it was the rage to have websites that were 'sticky'. The 'stickiness' refers to the ability of your website to retain the interest of the users and keep them coming back for more. In some areas of commerce and entertainment it is still a valid objective to keep people coming back to your website to spend time viewing and interacting with the content.

For many business websites, however, I question the validity of the premise that you want or need your website to be sticky. Is it of value to your business to have people wandering around the foyer browsing your brochures for extended periods and on a regular basis? The physical inconvenience notwithstanding, I don't think this sort of activity will help many businesses.

Remember why you are in business, and what it takes for your business to be successful. If having people 'browsing' does nothing for your bottom line, don't focus on it as you design and develop your website.

Exceptions to this rule may include some retail sites where it can be of value to have people dropping in for a browse and an 'impulse buy'. Amazon.com entices the user to become absorbed in the whole consumer cycle. It can be a real test of character to drag yourself away from that website without keying in your credit card number.

In the words of Homer Simpson, 'Mmmmm, books.'

For the rest of you, concentrate on getting the user to take action that is of benefit to you, such as calling your sales team or visiting your showroom.

Benchmarking

In many facets of business and life, we use benchmarking to judge our performance.

> 'How does my house compare with the Jones's?'

> 'How does my car compare with a Mercedes?'

In both of these examples the values of the house and car in comparison is clear. The house has five bedrooms and the car has five drink holders.

The problem that arises when comparing one website with another is that the real value of another website to that business is not clear when you look at the website. It is easy to assume that because a website looks nice, or has lots of 'bells and whistles', it adds value to the company it represents. This assumption is based on nothing but supposition.

A website might look good but:

> The look and feel runs counter to the company's branding objectives.

> The company has spent its budget on a new image and what their customers really want is a system whereby they can log in to read their current trading reports.

> The site has not been properly registered with the search engines and no one out of the industry can find it.

> The content on the website is out of date or wrong or both.

> The target audience for the website will not use the website because they cannot find the content they are after due to the way the content is presented.

> An important audience group are people living in remote areas, but they find the site impossible to use due to the time it takes to load on their PCs.

I recently had an experience that emphasised the difficulty of assessing the value of a website to its owner. I was putting some information together for a company that was looking at developing a new website. A key driver for the development was a gap analysis they had performed between their current situation, and the website of their major competitor.

I won't worry about specifics here, but suffice to say, three weeks later that major competitor contacted my office for support in redeveloping their website. Why? Because the website was out of date. It was of little value to their customers. The information they were publishing was a waste of time as nobody used it. And to top it off, they hated the look and feel of the whole thing and regretted their decision to build it in the first place.

Naturally, I did not mention the experience to either party. For me however it was a lesson learned.

Saying that you like the look of a website, or that you want a component that works like a component on another website, is a good way of defining what your solution should look/work like. However, make sure you work out what your website should include based on your business needs, before you get too focused on copying ideas from elsewhere.

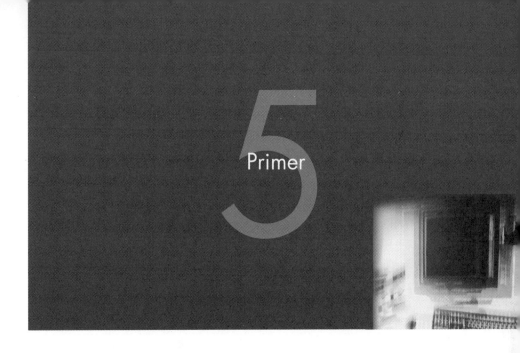

5 Primer

Half-hearted efforts

In the interest of having at least a contact presence on the Internet, some businesses put a simple one or two page website up. Fine. The problem is that often, nay, usually, these websites look as cheap as they are.

I have an issue with tacky websites that are there just for the sake of being there. This is not too difficult an argument for me to push either. If most people want to get a snapshot of a business, they do so using the Internet first and foremost. The vast majority of people also say that what they see on the Internet is how they perceive the business to be. (After all, what other reference point do most of us have?)

My advice is that if you are going to have a website, large or small, make sure it presents your business as you would like others to perceive it.

Sometimes websites have 'Under construction' signs as an indication of things to come. Once upon a time it was thought sensible that domain names that were taken should lead to websites 'under construction'. This may have been to demonstrate that the domain name is taken. It may have been to grab a slice of the World Wide Web pie. (I know it feels good to have something/anything there!) Either way it was and is a waste of time and effort that should be focused on your business.

Do not use 'Under construction' signs. Users of the Internet know they are a cop-out. If something is not ready to go to air, don't publish it at all. Yes, there are some examples where it is great to give advance warning of an exciting development or revelation. 'Under construction' signs are tantamount to giving your prospect a glossy brochure about your business that contains only blank pages.

By the way, signs like 'Coming soon' and 'Watch this space' are equally useless.

See what I mean:

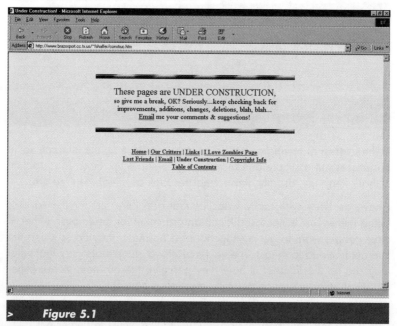

> **Figure 5.1**

Under construction pages are a waste of everybody's time.

A phased delivery

Budget

One of the great showstoppers for any business project, IT or otherwise, is the budget. Some organisations fall into the trap of letting their website project become a major hurdle because they try to achieve too many things at once. There is nothing wrong with breaking the website project into a number of phases. Often the more complex and expensive elements can be deferred to phase two.

Which bits do you do first? Hopefully the bits that are going to bring you benefits. In general, your business will need to establish a professional and appropriate presence on the web. This probably means you should get the website design organised and the fundamental content elements in place. From here you need to work out what extra functions your target audience wants. Is it detailed product and technical information? Is it the ability to place orders via an extranet? Is it the ability to access your databases?

Work out the priorities, then see how they match up against the budget. Plan to deliver on the priorities over a period that will fit in with your budgetary limitations.

> **Hint:**
> *If you can deliver real cost savings (or revenue gains) in phase one, then you can pay for phase two. For example, put some user and technical documentation on your website instead of sending it with every product sold. This might save you thousands of dollars every month.*

Panic jobs

A sure-fire way to upset everyone is to try to squeeze ten weeks worth of work into four weeks. Too often businesses leave themselves exposed by trying to fit web projects into timelines that are just not feasible.

Often, the driver behind the hurried development of a website is the presentation of some key information to launch a new product, brand or business entity. In my experience, most last-minute panic jobs can be managed with some thought and discussion with regard to what is really required by the due date. Again it comes down to an understanding of the objectives of the exercise.

If the company is launching a new entity and with it a new domain (website) address, it may be quite feasible to offer the bare bones of the website by the due date. By providing some fundamental information such as company background, product and service descriptions and contact details, the website can cater for the majority of short-term requirements.

This may take the pressure off you and the web provider, and allow you to focus on the careful and considered delivery of the total solution.

Please note that I did not suggest a solution that looks 'half-baked'. If people are coming to your website and being confronted by something that looks amateurish and sloppy, then that is how they will perceive your organisation. That is not the objective of the exercise I am sure.

CRM

'CRM' stands for Customer Relationship Management. The most overused and abused term in the free world today. CRM refers to the activities that allow businesses to understand the behaviours of their customers. It extends from managing customers who call your premises, managing the activities of your sales force and measuring website traffic flow, through to understanding your customers' needs by analysing their purchasing behaviours and demographic profiles over an extended period of time.

I'm mentioning CRM here because more than once I have seen a web project stymied because management wanted to integrate a CRM system into the project, but no one could actually articulate what they were after. There are of course software vendors who will gladly sell you solutions ranging from $500 to $5 million to manage your CRM. Like all things, you need to understand your CRM needs and purchase accordingly.

CRM systems do interface with your website, and you can manage your website's responses to individual queries or actions using CRM intelligence software. But my advice to you is to worry about CRM after you have got your website up and running, unless you are building a large B2C website with plenty of cash and a well defined business model.

Here are some ways to understand your customers without buying CRM software:

> Well-designed websites will cater for the needs of your target audiences.

> Websites can deliver a degree of personalisation without CRM software. (Check out the section on personalisation on page 39.)

> You can collect plenty of information about your customers' online behaviours and see how users move around the website by looking at the website traffic reports. Identify separate content elements that are of interest to the same group of users.

> Analyse the results of surveys you publish. The surveys can be used to gather personal preferences, or to identify trends amongst a particular audience or interest group (for example, everyone who reads a particular article or document).

> If your online store is set up well, that is, it caters for the needs of your business, you should know who your customers are, what their preferences are, and how you can entice them to purchase more in the future. Add your own questions to the form they complete when they purchase your products. Get their email address as part of the transaction (standard protocol) and email them a follow up survey after the sale has been completed.

Most CRM systems are separate from the fabric of the website. Very few website projects need to be held up to wait for the CRM system and functionality to be finalised. If you are not convinced, have a word with your CRM vendor (if CRM is on the table there is probably a vendor in the pie somewhere).

Keeping your website current

One of the difficulties many companies face is maintaining the content on their websites. For some websites, the content does not change or does so rarely. Other websites have changes that occur infrequently, and others have content that is continually changing.

You must take the frequency of changes that occur in your business into account when you design your website. If your product line is continually changing then you had better be prepared to keep it current on your website. If your company is rapidly expanding and opening offices in new areas, then you had better plan for this with your website.

The most disappointing example of a website that has not kept pace with the business is a website that features a monthly newsletter that is six or even 12 months out of date. Often this occurs because the company has not considered the process of maintaining this part of the website. Sometimes it is because the company forgets to update the content, and in many cases it is because the IT department of the company has been too busy to update the content. Most IT departments have other more important fish to fry than updating the wording on a website.

No excuse is a good excuse for content that is wrong.

When you are completing the Website Planner you will be asked to note how often each element of content on your website is likely to require updating. This will tell you (and your web provider or technical staff) how you will need to approach managing the content of the site.

There are a number of ways to manage content that is continually changing. In my opinion the best way to manage this sort of content is to have a content management application that allows staff to do it, without the intervention of IT or web people. There are a lot of content management applications (and options) available. Indeed many companies have spent way too much money on systems they really didn't need. Web professionals can whip up a content management application for textual content such as news, press releases, and product catalogues, for a very reasonable price.

Take this requirement into consideration early and your web provider can build the required system for you.

Systems like this can be developed using rapid application development software like Cold Fusion in two to three weeks, providing the customer with an easy to use tool that allows them to update the content of their website in real time.

Personalisation

Personalisation as a concept was very popular in the late 1990s; of late however it has become less of a fad, and highly relevant in certain circumstances.

Personalisation refers to the ability of a website to recognise the user and respond to their personal needs accordingly. There are typically two 'methods' of personalisation.

Explicit personalisation

This refers to the process whereby the visitor to the website enters the name and password, then gets to view content that is of express interest to them. In this scenario they get to nominate what content they see on their personal version of the website, as well as access to any personal records they may have that are linked to the website.

Typically, Intranets and password-protected areas on websites offer this functionality—a unique user experience that fulfils the expressed needs of that user.

Intranets and websites with secure access for staff are becoming very popular, and for good reason. Companies are finding that if they present information to their staff in a logical and efficient way, whilst giving their staff more power over what they view and when, they will increase productivity and morale. Now staff are logging into a website by name and password, and are seeing all of their professional and personal information displayed before them on one 'digital desktop'. In the one view you might see incoming emails, general company news, news specific to your role in the organisation, your chosen news of the world, and links to other content and applications that you are likely to need. This format gives the company a platform through which they can readily communicate information to employees in the most effective way.

Websites with this sort of personalisation are often entertainment, media and finance sites. They may or may not have a user-pays or subscription model regulating user access.

Implicit personalisation

Personalising a website implicitly refers to the process of presenting content that the user is likely to want, based on established norms and behavioural patterns of other users of similar profile. It does take some smarts and database technology, but systems can develop a blueprint for the patterns of commonly displayed behaviours on websites. If 90% of visitors to the website go from an article on snow skiing to the section with the weather report in it, the system might put a link to the weather report on the same page as the skiing article (oversimplified example but you get my drift).

The challenge is to justify the value of such systems within the business website context. It is likely that because the software vendors discovered ways to deliver personalisation, they were a primary force behind its popularity. Now the focus is on the explicit needs of businesses and not the technologies available. You need to ask:

What sort of personalisation are you going to have on your website?

_____

_____

Why will this personalisation benefit your business?

_____

_____

_____

_____

_____

_____

Ask your customers

Get another opinion—ask your customers

One of the best sources of information on your company is your current customer. They know what it's like to deal with you. They know why they prefer to deal with you. They will have a certain view of what you and your company represent. They probably know quite a bit about your competitors. Many of them will have done a comparative analysis between you and your competitors. Your customers are also going to know how you can improve your service using your website.

With all of this knowledge so close, can you afford not to get their input into what you are doing with your website?

Tell your customer what you are doing and get their opinions on matters that will affect website design. Find out what they think would be important content for them if they were not trading with your company. Ask them why they like to do business with you. Can you portray this in your online branding?

Don't spend thousands on formal market research; ask your top ten customers a handful of questions each over a cup of coffee. Let them talk.

You might learn a whole lot more than you bargain for. This is not just to support your website; it is for your business.

Find out how they perceive your company

How do they perceive your position in the market?

How is your company compared with your competitors?

What style do they associate with your company?

Do they see your company as new, old, stable, changing, cheap and cheerful or blue chip?

The answers to these questions will help you understand where you are in reality.

_____

_____

_____

_____

_____

_____

_____

_____

Improved communications

Ask your customers if there are any communications they would like to streamline using the Internet.

Would they like to see their private price lists on your website?

Would they like to be able to book services or order products via the website?

Do they want access to technical documents or manuals on the website?

What else do they want?

_____

_____

_____

_____

_____

_____

Don't be frightened by this. You are just fact finding for now. If your customers ask for something that is too expensive or just not on your radar, at least you will know what is on their minds. You might even get a hint of what your competitor is offering them in this space.

Ask them what it was that made them use you in the first place.

_____

_____

_____

_____

_____

_____

(This will help you to understand what it is that you need to do or portray to get other customers.)

> Food For Thought

If word of mouth is the greatest driver of customers to your business, it makes sense to try to enhance what you are offering to your existing customers so that the word of mouth dynamic is enhanced.

I was in a meeting recently, talking to representatives from a company that ran a chain of vehicle service centres. They were considering their approach to marketing their company on the Internet. They had market research evidence that customers chose their service centres through word of mouth.

'People need to be living or working close to their service centre. Apart from that it comes down to who's got the best reputation.'

It made sense to me.

These guys would be best served by cranking up the word of mouth factor by offering better service to their existing customers. Publish service records; email the customers news about their car or about special deals on products for their car. Send them a reminder when their service is due and offer to provide free wiper blades if they book before a certain date. Provide the option to book online. (If they do, send them a return email confirming their booking and saying thank you.) They can and should still have a professional website for their business, but it could well be this focused activity that brings the real rewards.

What is the website for?

Set your objectives—what is the website for?

Only you (and your staff) can answer this question with respect to your website. The answer will form the basis of your approach to the rest of this project.

Some possible objectives

Prospecting

> To promote the business and to attract new customers

> To provide customers and others with a way to contact the business

> To display our credentials to prospects

> To improve our public image using the Internet

> To showcase the work of the business

> To provide staff, customers and prospects with up to date information regarding the business.

Process improvement

> To sell our products or services online

> To provide the investor community with information about the business

> To comply with the requirements of the ASX

> To download information to reduce the number of calls and requests we get for this information

> Link to systems to provide users with information held in databases and other systems

> To provide an online booking or ordering facility

> To provide an access point for staff to log in and get information when they are away from the office.

Client management

> To provide existing customers with detailed product information

> To provide clients with information via a secure log in facility

> Link with other backend systems to present clients with information about their trading.

General

> To develop a sense of pride in the business and the website.

Do not tick my examples; write your own. By all means use mine as a guide but think in terms of what your business needs. Write down your objectives here:

The company website is for:

1. _____

_____

_____

2. _____
_____
_____

3. _____
_____
_____

4. _____
_____
_____

5. _____
_____
_____

6. _____
_____
_____

Who is the website for?

Identify your target audience/s

This will tell you what you need on the website.

Who are you aiming this website at?

Why will these target audiences use the website?

What do you want them to do?

How best can you help them do what you want them to do?

Have they any special needs?

> **Example target audience**

(for Funky Monkey Furniture Company)

Who are they?
> Furniture buyers in companies. ▶

What do they want to do?
> Check our company credentials.
> Look through our catalogue of furniture.
> Review our prices, terms and delivery times.
> Contact our sales office.
> Contact our design office.
> Contact our service division.
> Visit our showroom.

What do you want them to do?
> Look at our website and contact our sales people.
> Be impressed with our catalogue and call us without wasting our time asking for prices.
> Read the Handy Hints section rather than calling the service department asking time-consuming questions about furniture care.
> Visit our showroom and talk with our sales people.

What do you need to provide to achieve this?
> Well-presented case studies (including virtual tours).
> Talk about our processes and what makes us unique/special.
> Good photos of furniture.
> Easy to use contact details for sales and other departments.
> Good Handy Hints and FAQ section.
> Provide showroom address and contact details.

Target Audience 1

Who are they?

_____

_____

What do they want to do?

_____

_____

_____

_____

What do you want them to do?

_____

_____

_____

_____

What do you need to provide to achieve this?

_____

_____

_____

_____

Target Audience 2

Who are they?

_____

_____

What do they want to do?

_____

_____

_____

_____

What do you want them to do?

_____

_____

_____

_____

What do you need to provide to achieve this?

_____

_____

_____

_____

Target Audience 3

Who are they?

_____

_____

What do they want to do?

_____

_____

_____

_____

What do you want them to do?

_____

_____

_____

_____

What do you need to provide to achieve this?

_____

_____

_____

_____

Target Audience 4

Who are they?

_____

_____

What do they want to do?

_____

_____

_____

_____

What do you want them to do?

_____

_____

_____

_____

What do you need to provide to achieve this?

_____

_____

_____

_____

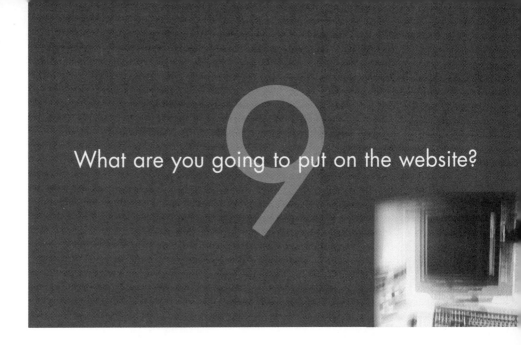

What are you going to put on the website?

OK, it's time to work out what you are going to have on your website. My advice: forget the websites with snazzy interactive games, flash splash screens, banner advertising and links to www.amazon.com. Put what your business needs on the website.

Let's have a crack at some standard stuff here. Remember that I don't know your business. These are some standards that seem to do the trick in most but not all cases. Keep an eye open for special items that I have not mentioned that you could use on your website.

Company information

People will want to know what you are about before they are going to do business with you. Don't think this is not so. This section is your first shot at getting your prospects to develop an affinity for your company. Call it trust, call it familiarity; people want to feel comfortable before they spend.

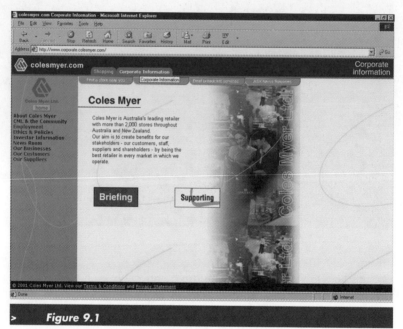

Coles Myer provides a comprehensive view of the company through their Corporate Information section.

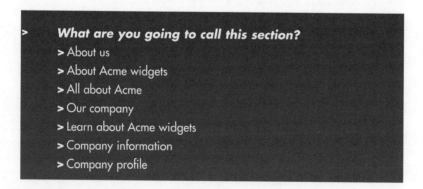

> **What are you going to call this section?**
> > About us
> > About Acme widgets
> > All about Acme
> > Our company
> > Learn about Acme widgets
> > Company information
> > Company profile

Now, what else do you want to include in the company information section? Check out some example headings here:

> .

Company history
> Our history
> Looking back
> History of Acme widgets
> Company history
> Origins of Acme widgets

Company ownership
> Our owners
> Company ownership

Company structure
> Organisational structure
> Our staff
> Company structure

What makes you special
> Uniquely Acme
> Why Acme is special
> Acme—a cut above

Key staff
> Our staff
> Key staff
> Executive team
> Board members
> Our people

What company information do you want on the website? List the items and expand on them here. How many pages will each piece of content require?

_____

_____

_____

_____

_____

_____

_____

_____

_____

_____

_____

_____

Investor information

> Possible headings:
> For investors
> Investor information
> Investor details

If the company is listed, the website is the most logical place to publish information to comply with the requirements of the ASX.

> Publish your annual reports.
> Publish your share price (in real time).

To service the investor community you should publish information that will give them a good idea why they should invest in you. Tell them why your company is a safe bet for the short and longer term.

If you have a strong executive group or Board of Directors, talk about their strengths.

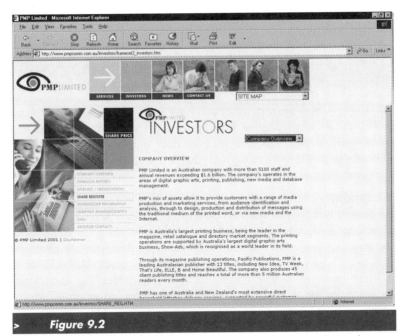

> **Figure 9.2**

PMP Limited provides a comprehensive 'Investor' section on their website.

**Is investor information required on the website?
If so, what do you want to include?**

_____

_____

_____

_____

_____

_____

Product and services information

Tell visitors to your website what you have to offer. People are out there in their droves searching for that special someone with whom they can do business. If they walk through your door and you don't show them what you've got, they'll turn right around and walk back out again. _Show them what you've got!_

The thinking on how much product and service information you should put on your website has shifted. I believe that unless you are in a business consulting field, you should tell the world everything. If a potential customer can go to your website and make up their mind to purchase from you, based on the information presented, great. The website is different from the Yellow Pages because it provides the opportunity for the customer to make a purchasing decision, as opposed to just informing the customer of what your company offers. Show people how and why your product or service works, what it takes to purchase that product or service and, if appropriate, how much it costs. Ideally your target market will decide not to look any further and beat a path to your door, money in hand.

Some companies prefer not to publish too much detail in case it stops the prospect from contacting them. They feel that when they are face to face with a prospect they are likely to be able to talk them around into buying, whereas the website may have given the prospect sufficient reason not to call. If what's on your website accurately reflects your business position and someone does not call because of that position, you have just saved the effort of qualifying them as a viable prospect.

As a user of the Internet, if I am looking for something and find just what I want on a company's website, I am going to contact them first. Sometimes the clincher is in the detail.

Some businesses have hundreds or even thousands of products in their catalogues. The challenge for these companies is publishing this information to the web. The good news is that if those companies have the product information held in a database, it should be possible to take a feed from that database and publish the information to the website. The trick can be getting the products into the database and keeping them current in there. There are numerous database solutions available to manage product information, and nearly all of them are web-friendly.

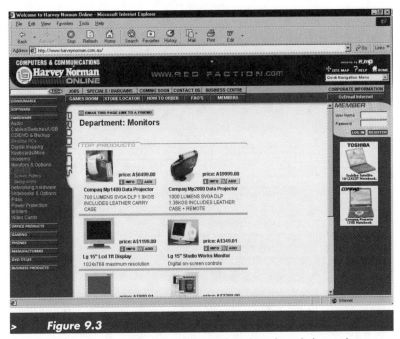

> ### *Figure 9.3*

Harvey Norman sells a limited range of products through their website.

Many consultants don't like telling the world too much because they fear someone will 'steal' their ideas. I can understand the fear; it doesn't make sense to tell the world about any specific proprietary methodologies you have developed that have become your unique selling proposition. It also doesn't make much sense to give the world so much information that they do not need to acquire your services. The way to get around this is to provide some case studies. Let the reader know the sorts of issues involved and the positive outcomes achieved. The prospect will be able to recognise cases that mirror their own needs. (More on case studies in a moment.)

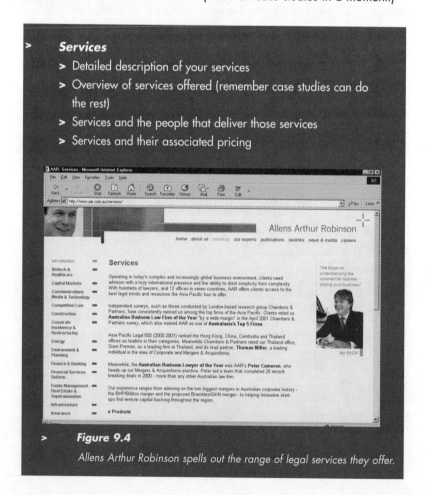

> ### *Services*
> > Detailed description of your services
> > Overview of services offered (remember case studies can do the rest)
> > Services and the people that deliver those services
> > Services and their associated pricing

> **Figure 9.4**
> *Allens Arthur Robinson spells out the range of legal services they offer.*

> **Products**
> > Your products in all of their variations
> > A list of specials
> > A limited range of products that you know will sell online
> > Exactly what you stock in your physical retail stores
> > The most popular items you hold in your physical stores
> > Products you want to sell quickly
> > Products with or without their pricing

What product/service information do you want on the website?

How detailed will the information be?

Why does your decision work best for your business?

Now answer these questions for your business.

_____

_____

_____

_____

_____

_____

_____

_____

_____

_____

Shopping cart

You've listed the products you want to sell, now you need a mechanism for selling them online. You need to spend time trying out the various shopping carts available. The best way to do this is to go through the process of buying things from other websites (stop short of submitting your credit card details).

If you were selling relatively low-value items in large quantities online, I would recommend using one of the large commercial gateways such as provided by the big banks or Camtech. Think in terms of minimising your risk and maximising the security. People are steadily becoming more attuned to shopping by credit card on the Internet, but they are also listening for bad press. Make sure you are dealing with a big player that has guarantees covering the transactions (check with your bank).

If you are selling high-value items, think twice about bothering to sell them over the Internet. Is the effort worth it? Are you setting up a facility that no one is likely to use? By all means use your website to show customers what you have to offer, and then use it to organise your appointments to demonstrate your offerings, but don't try to sell boutique high-value items over the web unless your are prepared to manage the returns. Better still; see how you go with the following e-tailing questionnaire.

E-tailing questionnaire

E-tailing refers to the process of selling your goods or services (or whatever) via an online transaction. One upon a time the term e-commerce sort of fit this bill. Now e-commerce encompasses many facets of communications and is enveloped by acronyms and associated terms that continue to emerge from everywhere. E-tailing transactions usually involve the use of credit cards, and some organisations take other 'currencies' such as smartcards and digital cash or coupons. (For more information on the various online payment vehicles have a look at www.whatis.com. Start with 'e-tailing' and see where it takes you.)

I have seen too many examples of small- to medium-sized businesses waste their time and money trying to sell their goods and services online. Before you commit your company to selling anything online I would ask you to work through the following questions. These questions are designed to make you focus on some of the potential shortfalls that you might face in this area.

1> Do you sell a product or service that people will want to purchase online?

2> What is the benefit to your customers of purchasing your products or services online?

3> Where are the customers who are going to buy your products or services online located? Are they local, regional, interstate or overseas?

4> How will you ship your products or deliver your services to customers when they order them online from a distance?

5> Who is going to prepare the goods you sell online for dispatch and distribution? Will you need to commission a (fulfilment) company to do this?

6> What is your current rate of returns on goods sold? How do you manage returns now? (Does the customer bring them back to the store?) Given this rate of returns, and factoring issues such as damage in transit and late delivery, how will you manage returns of purchases made from remote or distant locations?

7> What effect does the knowledge and consultative approach of your sales people have on the value of the purchase, the suitability of the purchase, the rate of returns and credits, and the lifetime value of the customer? If this direct contact is removed, how do you think it will affect your sales figures and costs?

8> To what degree are the products you sell generic? Will the customer know exactly what to expect when they open the box? If the products you sell are generic, and you and others are selling them online and offline, why do you think the customer will buy them from you online? On the other hand, if the products are unusual, unique and likely to be something of a surprise when the purchaser opens the box, what proportion of purchasers are going to be dissatisfied and want to return the goods? Products that are textural such as clothing, floor coverings, soft furnishings and curtains can be very difficult to represent online. It is a precise science and requires specific skills to make images look like the real thing. Different computer configurations can represent colours differently. 'I ordered green, not aqua!' or how about, 'This cushion is way too firm for Fluffy!' Textures can also be very difficult to portray/describe.

9> How is the cost of selling your goods online, packing the orders, distributing the goods and managing your usual rate of returns going to affect the price you charge for your products, and the profit you make?

10> If you have a shop, store, or chain of stores, what percentage of your sales (and your profits) come from incidental sales that occur when customers are in your stores? Will these incidental sales continue if you sell online? How? (Don't even think about the Amazon model unless you are prepared to invest heavily.)

11> If your business is a franchise and you have established area-based franchise agreements with the franchisees, what system will you use to apportion the sale to the franchise owner in the region concerned?

12> If your products are sold in retail stores run by other companies (such as Target, Bunnings, David Jones) what percentage of your products are sold because they have a presence in these stores? Are your precision drill bits sold where drills and other tools are sold? Are people attracted to those stores because your drill bits are there, or because they stock drills and are likely to stock a range of precision drill bits?

13> How many of your drill bits are sold to buyers who went to the store to buy hammers but happened to see your products on the shelf? Is your product usually an incidental sale or does it drag people into the shops?

Case study—Funky Monkey Furniture (FMF)

FMF were very excited about selling their furniture online. The idea of having hundreds of businesses keeping their factory at fever pitch was very appealing. However, when they did their research they identified the following issues:

1> The vast majority of FMF sales were generated by the ability of their consultants to analyse the needs of their customers and design furniture solutions accordingly.

2> 20% of FMF customers gave them 80% of their sales and virtually none of their headaches. It was their attention to customer service and developing strong face to face working relationships that drove their repeat orders and referrals to new customers.

3> Selling FMF furniture involves a painstaking assessment of textures, colours and shapes. FMF customers are generally very particular about quality, form and function. FMF prides itself on providing a working and living experience more than it does on selling items of furniture.

4> FMF furniture is made on demand and according to the explicit needs of the customer. To sell items online meant that they would have to keep stock in a store ready for distribution, which would be very costly and risky. They could have considered making cheaper more generic lines but there are a number of competitors occupying this space.

5> FMF customers invariably pay their accounts on 30-day terms. Few of them would consider paying by credit card online.

6> The minimum value of an FMF item of furniture is $4,000 for an office chair.

7> An FMF consultant accompanies every item of furniture sold to the recipient to ensure that it arrives safely and that expectations are met.

Considering all of these facts, FMF management decided not to sell their products via a shopping cart on their website.

If you have managed to respond to all of the questions raised to your complete satisfaction, and you believe you have a genuine opportunity, fantastic. For 'How to' information, please consult the extensive range of textbooks on the subject in your local bookshop and talk to your web provider.

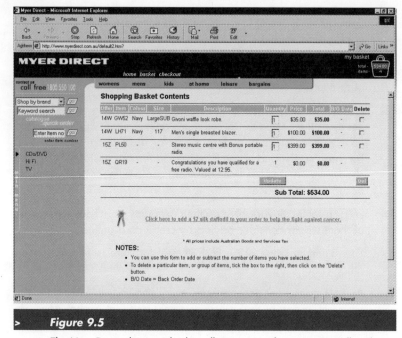

> ## Figure 9.5

The Myer Direct shopping basket tallies your purchases as you collect them.

Will you have a shopping cart on your website?
Why will it work for your business?

Case studies

Who can use case studies? Just about everyone. Web designers, software companies, consultants, builders, engineers, project managers, architects, advertising agencies, mining companies, publishers, training companies and a host of other company types can all get real value out of publishing their successes in the form of case studies.

I have spoken to a number of companies that have gained new business because a customer had seen a case study that sounded like what they were after. Case studies give the reader a sense that your company has a successful track record. If a prospect sees that you have expertise and experience in a particular field of interest, they are likely to want to sound you out. Sometimes the mere fact that you have been involved in a project of a particular nature is what sets you apart.

> This raises an important point. If you have experience or skills that might be considered specialised, the Internet can be your best friend. You can market these particular skills and experiences effectively because, if people need to track down such specialist skills, they are likely to go to a search engine and enter the skills in question. You must be ready. If I want to find someone who specialises in cutlery design, I am going to enter 'cutlery design' into my favourite search engine.
>
> If you as a cutlery designer, have registered your website with the popular search engines, and have included 'cutlery design' in the registration information and in the metadata on your website, I will find you! (More on search engines in Chapter 4—Bringing people to your website on page 28.)

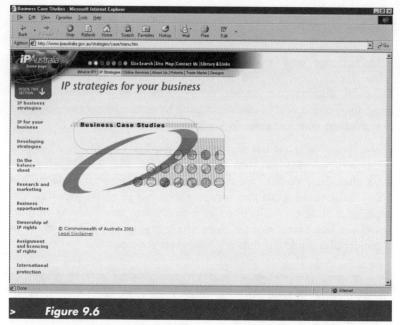

> **Figure 9.6**

IP Australia uses case studies to demonstrate the successful projects they have completed.

Case studies effectively provide people with references up front. Readers can always check your bona fides by contacting the organisation mentioned in the case studies. In reality though, it is a very brave organisation that depicts work in a case study that they have never actually done. The readers of your case studies are likely to take what you include in the case studies at face value. That is why they are so powerful; not only do they indicate that your organisation can do what is represented in the case study, they also describe the context and relevance of that experience. Companies in construction and engineering can use case studies to effectively broadcast their skills in terms of physical work completed. The prospect will look at their case studies and immediately include them in the running for a project, even though they may not have heard of the company before.

*Will you put case studies on your website? Which ones and
how much detail will you include?*

_____

_____

_____

_____

_____

_____

_____

_____

_____

_____

_____

_____

Contact information

Regardless of what you are offering, you must tell the visitor to your
website how they can get in contact with you. Forget doing business
through an email form. If I want to discuss a big contract with a potential
supplier, I want to talk with a person.

Addresses, phone numbers and emails are the go. Give them an email
for sales, one for service, one for advice and so on. If you can, give them
the names of the people they can deal with in the particular part of your
business they want. If you've got staff working in different areas and at
different sites, publish all of the sites' contact details.

One more thing; don't hide the contact details. If I want to talk fast, I go
straight for the phone. (How about you?)

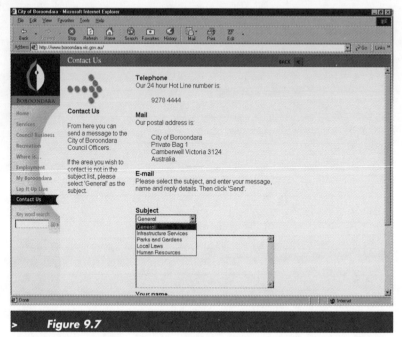

> **Figure 9.7**

City of Boroondara provides clear contact details. I like the way they use a drop-down menu to direct the email based on the subject of the email.

Once upon a time the thinking was not to have phone numbers and addresses on websites. (Who wants millions of people calling you or visiting your office? Let them use your website to do business. Just sit back and watch the Internet make you rich!)

We now know that the Internet is just another medium for communication, albeit a very effective one. Tell your prospects how they can get hold of you.

For your sake, don't force prospects to resort to the Yellow Pages to find you. They'll end up looking at a list that includes not just you, but all of your competitors too. From there it will come down to a price war (there go the margins!).

The 'Contact us' section of your website should be front and centre, one click away from the home page, if not on the home page. Put a 'Contacts' button in an obvious place.

> ### What contact information will you provide on the website?
>
> - Head office address and phone and fax numbers
> - Sales contact phone and fax numbers
> - Sales contact email addresses
> - Regional/other offices' or stores' addresses and phone and fax numbers
> - Customer support/service phone and fax numbers
> - Customer support/service email addresses
> - Public Relations/corporate affairs office contact phone and fax numbers and email address
> - Names and contact details for all senior management
> - Contact emails for the Board of Directors

Will you include names for some or all of these people so they can be contacted in person, or have generic position-based contacts such as sales@acme.com.au?

_____

_____

_____

_____

User forums

Once upon a time not too long ago everyone wanted a public forum on their website. It was to be a place where people could get together and talk about things related to the website and its business. This was all very well in theory, but the fact was that there were very few websites where people wanted to hang about chatting. The other issue for companies is what is being written in the forum. Just as members of the forum say nice things about your company, they can also damn it in the presence of your most treasured customers or prospects.

My inclination is that unless you are prepared to monitor the content of a public forum on a frequent basis, you shouldn't have one on your website.

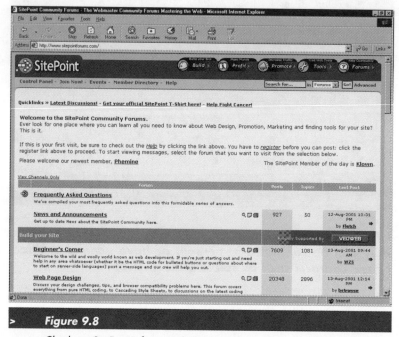

> **Figure 9.8**

Check out SitePoint's forums. They are a popular place for discussing websites.

Having said that, there is an area where a forum can be an effective tool for communication. Some companies are now including forums to facilitate internal communications. An example of this is within franchise organisations, where franchisees have a secure area on their website. Part of that secure area might be a forum where franchisees can discuss issues relevant to the business and their involvement. In such a case the forum may be an excellent vehicle for developing a sense of community amongst the franchisees, within which they provide each other with the support and advice they require for success.

Even an internal forum should be monitored however, to ensure that what is being published is in the organisation's best interests.

Will you put a forum on the website?

Who is it for?

Will it be available to the public or in a secure area?

How will it be monitored?

What value do you see the forum delivering?

_____

_____

_____

_____

_____

_____

Chat rooms

There are chat rooms all over the Internet. Like forums, chat rooms have been very popular on all sorts of websites. Like forums, they have been a waste of effort for the majority of business websites. Yes, there are plenty of chat rooms on entertainment and community-based websites that are used, but I would venture to say that of the total number of chat rooms placed on websites fewer than five per cent of them ever support decent productive dialogue. 'Hello, is anybody there?'

Do you want a chat room on the website?

Will it be in a secure area or available to the public?

Who is it for and why?

_____

_____

_____

_____

Feedback

This should be a simple email form. On your website the form should be accompanied by a statement saying that you would like to receive any constructive criticism about the website. You might be surprised how much value you can get from this. As a general rule people will tell you when you've made a mistake on your website. It is very unusual for people to send rubbish via this medium. (If it happens check with your cheeky neighbour or your ex-partner.)

If you get a bit of advice that is helpful, send back a quick thank you note. The person was on your site for a reason. They may well be a future customer; why don't you ask them in your 'thank you' email?

> *'Thanks for your comment Mary. We're making the change you pointed out. By the way, is there anything we can do for you? Did you find what you were looking for? Best wishes . . .'*

You never know where a sale might be lurking.

Will you have a feedback form on your website?

Who in your organisation is going to receive and act on the feedback received?

_____

_____

_____

_____

Virtual tours

Virtual tours are now used widely on a range of websites, and to good effect. I've used virtual tours for hotels, universities, shopping centres, houses for sale, and the insides of new vehicles. What better way to describe something than by holding the visitor's hand and showing them what they want to see?

There are a number of technologies used to support virtual tours. Some of them are simple, combining maps or text with still images. Others use technologies such as Ipix to provide the 360-degree experience. I have seen some virtual tours that feature all sort of links embedded within the 360-degree vision. Depending on your business and what you are trying to show visitors, your virtual tours can be as creative as you want.

For some examples of virtual tours check out www.ipix.com

> **Figure 9.9**

The South Australian Parliament has put together a virtual tour of their premises using the very popular Ipix system.

Like all aspects of your website, work out why a virtual tour would be good for your website. Then get out and explore the virtual tours on the Internet. Look at how different companies have presented their tours and used the technologies available. (I'll leave you to find them using your favourite search engine.)

Will you use a virtual tour on your website?

What will it be of?

How would you like it to work? (Assuming you have seen some on the Internet for comparison.)

_____

_____

_____

_____

_____

_____

News

Putting a news section on your website is a very good idea, the one proviso being that you or someone must keep it up to date (refer to Keeping your website current on page 38). News articles that provide updates on what is happening in and around your company can achieve a range of things:

> Visitors will see that the company is active and a viable entity with which they might do business.

> The 'News' section can act as a marketing tool to promote the good things about your company. The 'News' value tends to add credibility to items that might be interpreted otherwise as 'plugs' (sneaky).

> The 'News' section provides an excellent vehicle for keeping investors, clients, potential clients, staff and other parties abreast of what is happening in your organisation. ('I saw that you had success with the project with Acme Tools. We have been trying to do the same thing for months to no avail. When can you come and see us?')

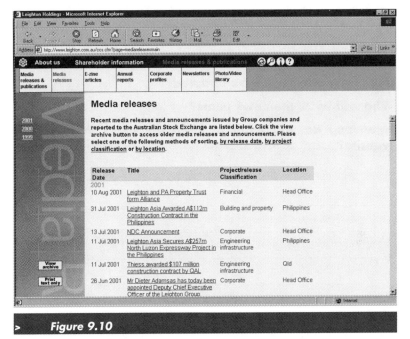

> **Figure 9.10**

Leighton really likes to promote their media releases online. They have plenty of releases available and the user can sort through the releases based on a range of criteria.

> **What sorts of news items will add value to your website?**
> > Product releases
> > New staff
> > Merger/acquisition information
> > Case studies
> > Relevant industry news

Will you have a News section on your website?

If so, how often will it be updated?

Who will write the news items?

How long do you want to keep the news items on the website?

_____

_____

_____

_____

_____

_____

_____

_____

Photo galleries

Depending on the type of business you are in, you may find a gallery on your website worthwhile. Examples of businesses that have galleries on their websites include:

> Architects

> Florists and plant growers

> Artists and sculptors

> Entertainers

> Event organisers

> Tattooists

> Sign-writers

Will you have a gallery on your website?

If so, what images will you put in it?

_____

_____

_____

White papers or technical information

Publishing white papers and technical documentation on your website can be very effective.

Recently, I met with a manufacturer of technical products who spent lots of time and money sending technical documentation to their distributor network and clients all over the world. The manufacturer knew full well that the majority of the documents sent were not read. (They had an email and phone customer support facility that effectively handled customer queries.) It had been their standard practice to distribute copies of the product documentation with every product sold. They even sent the documentation to prospective customers.

The solution to their problem seemed obvious. If they could reduce their spending on sending paperwork around the globe they would save potentially many thousands of dollars. I asked the person with whom I was speaking whether their distributors and customers were likely to use

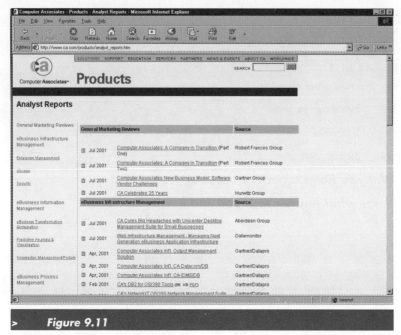

> **Figure 9.11**

Computer Associates recognise the value of displaying favourable product reviews on their website.

the Internet as a source of documentation. His reply was that both the distributors and customers had been screaming out for the information online. They didn't like getting the paperwork any more than the manufacturer liked sending it. The reason the company had delayed the website project was because there were so many issues involved and they had not had the resources (time) to throw at it.

A tactic in this situation might be to establish a simple website with barebones information on it, to publish the technical information. Tell the distributors and customers about it and update the documentation when appropriate. Such a website may not win 'beautiful website of the year', but it might save heaps of money and make everybody's lives easier.

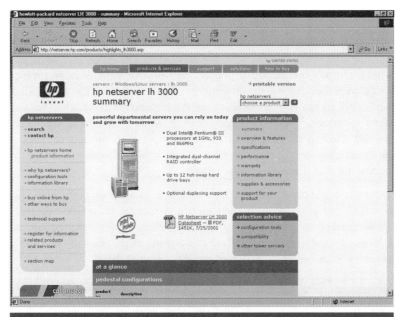

> **Figure 9.12**

Hewlett Packard provides as much technical information as you could want
to make a purchasing decision.

**Will you put technical documents or product or service
related documents on your website?**

If so, what types will you include?

**Who will write these documents or where will they come
from?**

_____

_____

_____

_____

_____

_____

Information from internal systems and databases

I have already mentioned a phased delivery for your website project. More often than not it is the integration of databases into the website that waits until phase two. Depending on the databases or systems that you want to access, the project may take a while and cost a significant amount. Having said that, businesses that have their product catalogues in databases can greatly enhance the value of their websites by publishing that database content there.

There are some databases that hold real-time information relevant to your business that your target audiences are desperate to see. Whether it's stock market information, traffic information, sales information, or information specific to your industry or organisation, you may be able to enhance your business by publishing it on your website.

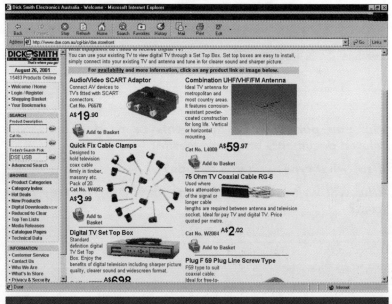

> **Figure 9.13**

Dick Smith Electronics has a huge catalogue of products. A database of these products and their availability feeds the website. Their website can even tell you which stores have the products available and which have run out.

Will you have data from your systems appearing on your website?

What data will be presented?

What systems will this data come from?

Information from other sources (syndicated)

The technology is here to allow you to grab information from external sources or websites, and publish it on your websites. Generally I am talking about textual content but it depends on your business. News and stock market information are the most common content types syndicated on websites. The process involves striking up an agreement with the organisation concerned, and some technical mucking about. Ask your suppliers how they would handle this for you.

The Excite.com.au website has news, weather, horoscope and stock market information on it. They syndicate all of this information from other sources. The information is then presented in the same style as the rest of the content on the website. At a glance it looks like Excite.com.au produces all of the information. This formatting of data to make it fit in with the style of your website is part of the syndication process.

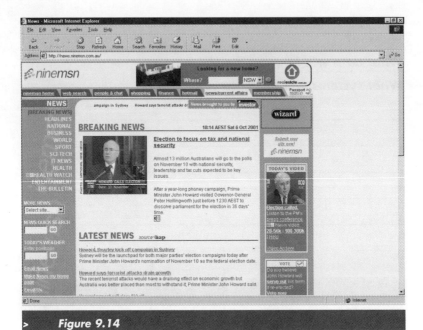

Ninemsn syndicates its up-to-the-minute news from AAP.

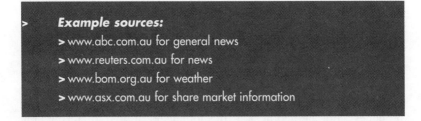

> **Example sources:**
> > www.abc.com.au for general news
> > www.reuters.com.au for news
> > www.bom.org.au for weather
> > www.asx.com.au for share market information

Will you have syndicated content on your website?

If so, what information do you want on your website?

Where will you get the content from?

_____

_____

_____

_____

Calendar information

Depending on their requirements some businesses should put calendars on their websites. Some examples include organisations that conduct seminars or feature events as part of their marketing or communications. There are other organisations that conduct product demonstrations on an ongoing basis, in a variety of destinations. Interested parties can access the website to find out the date of the demonstration/seminar most convenient to them. Sporting organisations may wish to include event fixtures on their websites. All of these examples will reduce the number of public inquiries that will have to be handled. In addition, the website can be equipped to manage the registration process, which further reduces the burden on staff.

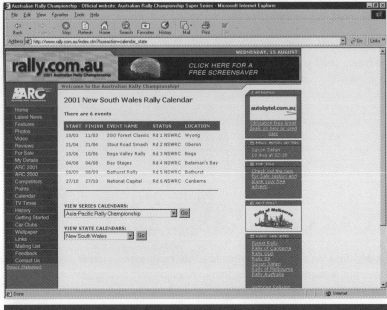

> **Figure 9.15**

The Australian Rally Championship provides calendars for each state and level of competition.

Will your website include a calendar?
If so, what will be listed on the calendar?

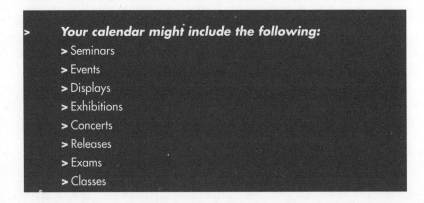

> **Your calendar might include the following:**
>   > Seminars
>   > Events
>   > Displays
>   > Exhibitions
>   > Concerts
>   > Releases
>   > Exams
>   > Classes

_____

_____

_____

_____

_____

_____

Secure client-specific information

Having a secure area on your website is not a major issue. The costs of having a secure area are not prohibitive, so if there is a business imperative to have one on your website, go ahead.

Users can access the website using either a generic or individual password. Generic passwords are not very secure, and the content on display will also have to be generic for all who access it. This may be suitable for businesses wanting to provide their own staff with information from remote locations. Individual passwords allow the display of information specific to the user. It also allows a more structured approach to managing access to restricted areas.

Franchise businesses or businesses with distributed staff can cheaply and securely distribute company information using a secure area on their website. The amount of information that can be distributed this way is without bounds. The amount of content on the secure area may be ten times greater than that on the rest of the website. The secure areas can contain information pertaining to:

> Human resources

> Contracts

> Leasing agreements

> Marketing and sales campaigns

> Sales and company reports

> Training information

Companies can put specific sales- or service-related information into a secure area for customer access. The customer can log in and see their own trading history and any other information that is relevant and of value.

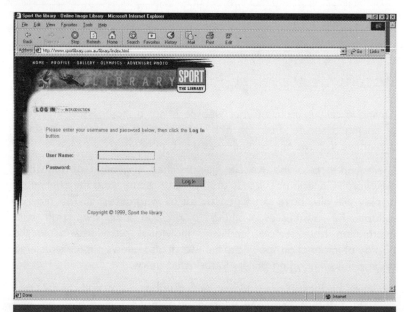

> **Figure 9.16**

Sport The Library provides a huge library of sporting images for their clients to peruse and purchase online. To manage the activity in their library they require that users must be registered before they are admitted to the library content.

Will you have a secure area on your website?

If so, whom will it serve, and why is it secure?

_____

_____

Maps

Maps can be used to demonstrate relevant information. Travel agents and others dealing with issues involving large tracts of land can use maps as effective means of communication. If your premises are off the beaten track, it might be sensible to include a map on your web-site. The same applies if you are 'hidden' somewhere in the suburbs.

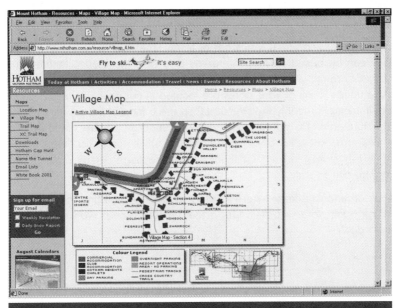

> **Figure 9.17**

Mt Hotham provides maps of the village and the surrounding areas on their website. Handy if you are going there for the first time and want to get to a particular lodge in the dead of night as the snow falls.

Will you use a map or maps on your website?

If so, what will they be of?

Who is likely to use the maps and why?

_____

_____

_____

_____

_____

_____

Store locator

Store locators can take a number of forms. They can be menu-driven or they can be based on maps. The key is to help the user to locate your store or branch without having to scroll through thousands of suburb or store names. If all of your stores are located in capital cities, use a drop-down menu to identify the city, and then use a map of the suburbs where the stores are. Do not use a map of the suburbs if there are only two stores in a particular city. If you have only five stores, list them. If you have fifty stores, do not list them all on one page; break them up by region, city or state.

Look around at different store locators in use. You will find them at most of the retail store websites. Get a feel for which ones work and which ones don't.

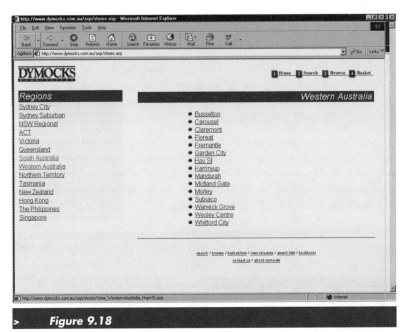

> ### Figure 9.18

Dymocks bookshops have a simple store locator on their website, broken down into states.

Will you use a store locator on your website?

If so, how will it be structured?

Can you find one on another website that you think would work on your website?

_____

_____

_____

_____

_____

Forms to submit information

Registration forms, application forms, requests for further information, surveys and other forms are good ways of developing a rapport with your targets. Mind you, if there is no perceived value for the user they will not fill the form in for the sake of it.

If your business demands that forms be filled out by your target audiences, then it is a good idea to publish them on your website where appropriate. The completed form data can be simply emailed back to your business to either be received as an email, or to go directly into a nominated database for further processing.

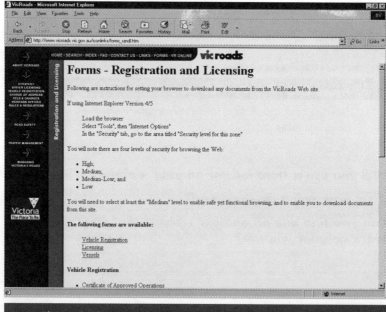

Figure 9.19

VicRoads provide all of their forms online in PDF format. Users can print the forms, fill them out and post them.

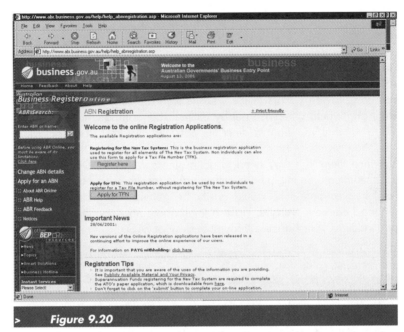

> **Figure 9.20**

The Australian Government Business Entry Point provides dynamic forms for
people and companies to request Tax File Numbers and ABNs online.

Designing forms and the email engines that service them should be no
problem for your web provider.

What forms will you use on your website?

Who will fill these forms out and why?

_____

_____

_____

_____

_____

_____

FAQ

Have a look at a few websites and see what they put in the Frequently Asked Questions sections. Depending on how you want to use the FAQs, you can provide visitors to the website with all of the information they want and would otherwise get by calling your company to ask. This is not to say that you want to deter the potential customer from contacting you. You want to provide them with the information they need to convince them that they need to do business with you. Depending on your situation, you might have considerable resources tied up answering calls from people who could easily be getting the information they require from your website. Have a think about how your website could add value to your business through the use of FAQs.

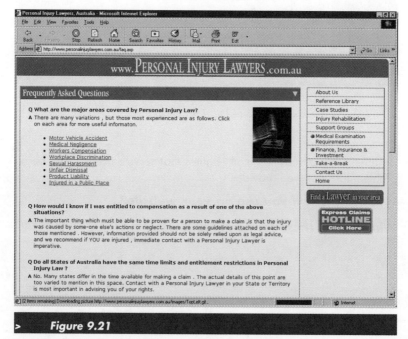

> **Figure 9.21**

The Personal Injury Lawyers website provides answers to frequently asked questions on their website.

The FAQ approach can readily be extended beyond the FAQ section of your website.

Any information that your business is often asked to provide should be considered for your website. If your business is constantly being called to provide educational information, consider compiling all of the relevant information and presenting it on your website under a 'For Schools' section. If investors tie up your switchboard, stick the relevant information on the website. Ditto for any information. Keep in mind that a growing proportion of people interested in your business will look at your website before calling you. If you can give them what they want during their first visit, you may save yourself and them a phone call.

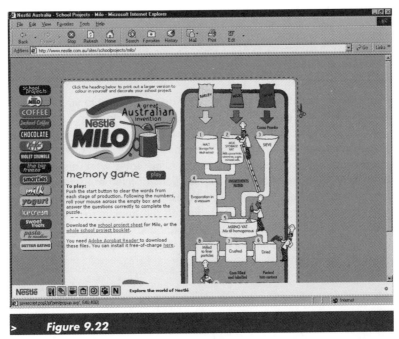

> **Figure 9.22**

Nestle provides a stack of information for school students to use in projects. I wish the Internet had been around when I was at school!

Will you have an FAQ section on your website?

Will you include other information such as a 'schools' section on your website?

_____

_____

_____

_____

_____

_____

Search

If your website contains a lot of information, you owe it to your visitor to show them to the department they want, without dragging them on a Cook's tour of your company first. I have heard arguments that it is good to make people read about your business before you give them the information they require. This smacks of slimy sales work and is totally out of kilter with the needs and expectations of Internet users. It is your duty (no less!) to help the visitor to whatever they want as quickly as you can. The Internet has completely redefined the meaning of 'time poor'. Users are not only time poor, they are 'wait intolerant'. If you can't give them what they are after very smartly, they'll be off somewhere else where they can get it.

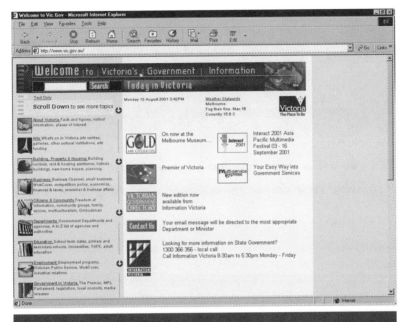

> **Figure 9.23**

The State Government of Victoria provides a prominent search facility to help users quickly find what they are after. For huge complex websites, a search facility is a must.

> **Food For Thought**

People are not necessarily impatient, it's just that we have all learned that if one website is hard work, we'll be able to find another that isn't. I won't go to the baker and wait in a long queue if I can duck into the supermarket next door and buy the equivalent loaf of bread in half the time. Chances are I'll go into the supermarket and end up purchasing bread of a lesser quality and be none the wiser. (No slight on supermarkets intended.)

See the analogy? Visitors to your website will wander off to your competitor's if they can't get what they want from yours.

> They may well end up doing business with your competitor as a result, and be blissfully ignorant of the fact that you could have provided them with a much better product or service.
>
> Have a surf around the Internet and see how different organisations present their search engines.

Will you use a search engine on your website?

If so, what style do you think would work for your website?

_____

_____

_____

_____

Surveys to capture responses

Depending on your personal experiences you may have differing ideas about the value, validity and even the tastefulness of surveying people who visit your website. I believe that surveys can be used as extremely effective means of helping your target audiences.

> Surveys can consist of as little as one short yes/no question.

> Surveys can ask users of your website what they think of a particular issue, product, service, or piece of content on your website.

> Surveys can be incorporated into forms that people fill out.

> Surveys can be used to ask users what they think of a website before changes are made.

> Surveys can be used on a new website to gauge the users' impressions.

> Surveys can capture user preferences relating to the way you conduct your business.

> Surveys can be used as a tool to help you to arrange the content on your website. (What is the most important content to have on this website?)

> Surveys can pop up in a window of their own, they can appear as a page on the website, and they can be emailed to the person concerned.

Organisations that are using surveys intelligently are capturing all sorts of valuable information from their target audiences.

Can you see how surveys might be of value to your organisation?

If so, how? List the sorts of surveys and outcomes that might be of value.

_____

_____

_____

_____

_____

_____

Employment opportunities

Here is another often-misused part of websites. What I read in this heading is that if I click on the heading, I will get a chance to look at any jobs that are available within the organisation. For this to happen though, the organisation must be prepared to update the job status on the website. Like any other piece of content that needs updating regularly, this can be subject to extreme delays and lack of commitment.

I have two recommendations for this section:

1> If your organisation does have a steady stream of job vacancies that applicants are likely to look for on your website, then get a content management application to publish them, so you don't have to worry the IT staff to do it for you. Remember that you will also need the HR staff and systems to manage the applicants that come through this window.

2> If you want potential applicants to make email inquiries, put a contact email address in the 'Contacts' section of the website. Again you will need to be able to support not only general inquiries, but also resumes that are sent through this medium. These inquiries need to be promptly managed and the appropriate responses sent. If you don't respond you won't look very good in the eyes of the applicant. As history has shown, today's job applicant is tomorrow's major prospect.

For many organisations, the idea of contacting job applicants without the intervention of recruitment consultants is a very attractive proposition. The truth for many though is they do not have the manpower or inclination to properly manage this channel.

If however, your organisation does have the ability to manage applications for work made online, ask yourself the following questions.

How would you like the system to work for you?

What sorts of applicants are you hoping to attract?

What information do you think these applicants will want to see on your website?

Is there any information the applicants might want that is not currently included in your website plan? If not, what is it?

_____

_____

_____

_____

_____

_____

Site map

If your website has any more than five pages of content in it, I would recommend you include a site map. A growing proportion of web users use site maps as their primary navigation tool. I must admit that when in doubt, I too reach for the site map. It does not have to be fancy: have a look around and see what others are doing. The site map should be full of links that allow the user to hop from your map straight to the page they are after.

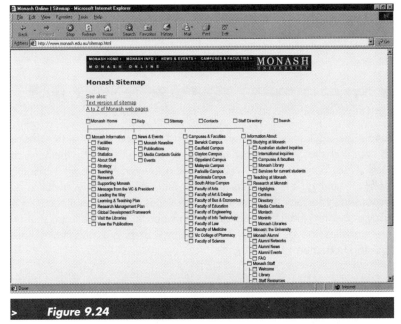

> **Figure 9.24**

Monash University has an enormous website. Their site map neatly lays out their website for quick access.

What sort of site map will you have on your website?

List some examples of site maps you have seen that you think will work well for your website.

_____

_____

_____

_____

_____

_____

Disclaimer

Bundle the disclaimer with any other legal stuff you might wish to have on your website. Rule number one: if you have any doubt whether you need a disclaimer on your website, ask a lawyer. Personally I like the idea of having a simple disclaimer that states that you take no responsibility for any unforeseen consequences or events that occur as a result of the information published on the website. Read the legal stuff on five websites in your industry and country of origin and make your decision from there.

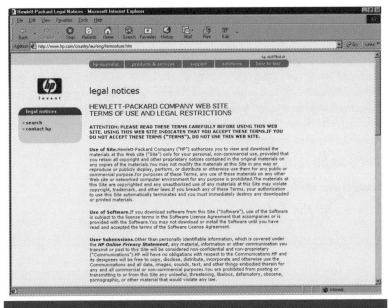

Figure 9.25

Hewlett Packard has a comprehensive section of legal information. They include a disclaimer, copyright information and more.

Do you need a disclaimer?

If so, what is it going to contain?

Do you need to include other legal notes such as copyright notices with the disclaimer?

Links page

Links pages provide access to other websites. Does this suit your business? Is it of value to have your users trundling off to your professional association where they can find alternative suppliers to your company? Depending on your business it might be quite viable. Have a look around; these days links pages are becoming fewer and fewer on business websites and websites in general.

Will you have a links page on your website?

If so, how will it benefit your organisation?

Where will the links go?

_____

_____

_____

_____

Website architecture

Determining the layout of the website can be a very tricky process. However, if you approach the issue now, you will dramatically improve your chances of getting it right.

If your target audience is coming to your website to get technical information, then you should ensure there are clear pathways to that information. If your target audience is coming to your website to get information and then register for something, you should design your website so they can step efficiently through the process, one click at a time. They should not have to get the information and then 'back out' of one section and look for the place to register. Think of it in terms of a physical model. The person walks into one office to find out about a product. To purchase that same product they then have to leave that building, walk a hundred yards, enter another building, catch a lift to the fifth floor, find the product they are after, and then buy it. Yuk!

Whether you are selling products online, or just providing information, the user's journey through your website should be aided in every way possible.

The trap many people fall into is setting up websites around the way your organisation is structured. Many websites demand that the user understand the structure of the organisation involved if they are to negotiate the website effectively. It takes a bit of role-playing to 'cleanse' your long-established understanding of your organisation from the process. (Think: 'I am the target audience; how can this website help me?')

The key is to put yourself in the shoes of your target audiences.

What do they want to do when they come to your website?

Which information are they going to want to access most frequently?

What are the logical or functional paths through your website content?

On a separate sheet of paper, have a go at mapping out your website. (Create your own site map.) Review it from the visitor's perspective.

_____

_____

_____

_____

_____

_____

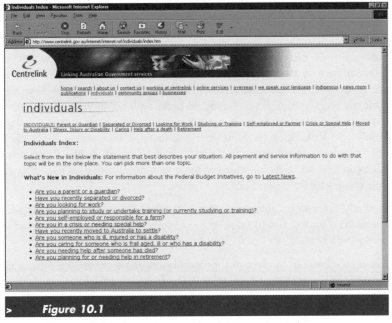

Figure 10.1

The Centrelink website is structured with its users in mind.

The Centrelink website is structured around life events. Visitors are able to work through their issues in a logical sequence to reach the required outcome. Put yourself in the position of someone who has just lost their job, and is looking for a new job. Check it out at:

www.centrelink.gov.au.

Notice that the website gives you all of the information and forms you require in a logical sequence.

Navigation

Navigation is closely tied to content architecture. The part which is relevant here is the headings businesses use on their websites. These headings must not be ambiguous. Nor can two headings be seen as remotely synonymous. If you have one heading leading your audience to 'Products', and another to 'Catalogue', then you have got it wrong. Surely your catalogue contains your products! If the catalogue contains special offers, then you are better off saying so in the headings. 'Catalogue' and 'Special offers' make much more sense as two distinct and complementary headings.

Similarly, 'Learning', 'Training for business' and 'Staff education' clash. Forget how well you and your staff understand the differences, the new person will not.

I've seen numerous tenders and project briefs come across my desk with the most basic clashes of terminology. The first thing I think is, 'well, these guys need help'.

If you are going to call in the web provider, my advice is to 'review' things like navigation headings and content architecture with them. If they have been around, they will pounce on the 'obvious' errors you have made.

Are the headings you're using in your site map unambiguous? Check them.

_____

_____

_____

_____

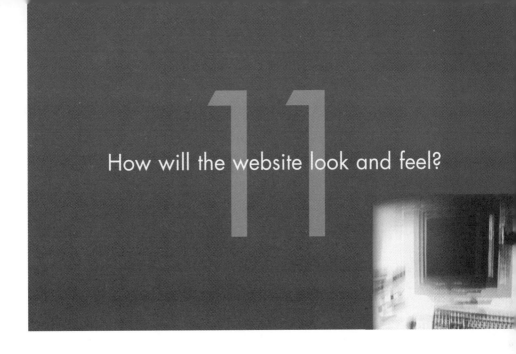

How will the website look and feel?

Knowing what your website should include and how it should work is one thing, knowing how it should look is another. I've said it before and I'll say it again, leave the designing to the designers. It can be very tempting to have a crack at designing your business website on the cheap. If you just grab the logo and stick it there, it will look as though it has been just grabbed and stuck there.

Making websites look good is no easier than making houses look good. It takes skill and an understanding of good design principles.

Now that I have persuaded you that you should not design the website yourself, I will confuse the matter by saying the designer cannot design the website without plenty of help from you. The designer needs to know what the website is going to include; hence you can give them a copy of this Planner when you have completed it. They will also want to know some touchy-feely stuff from which they will derive the principles underpinning your design.

Different designers approach projects differently, but I have given you some questions to get you moving in the right direction. Answer these questions and you will gain an insight into the thinking used by the designer in the development of the final design solution.

1>   What is the mission of your business? (If you have a mission statement, what is it?)

_____

_____

_____

_____

2>   What six words or phrases best describe the image you want to portray online?

Stable	Solid	Quick	Big
Friendly	Sharp	Valuable	Small
Caring	Motherly	Technical	Global
Warm	Secure	Dynamic	Wealthy
Progressive	Experienced	Personal	Sophisticated
Traditional	Discreet	Cold	Contemporary
Groovy	Stylish	Conservative	Rational
Green	Committed	Casual	Suave

Choose some of mine or use your own. Think about what your business should represent.

_____

_____

_____

_____

_____

_____

Rank the six adjectives in importance if you can. 'Above all else, our business is . . .'

3> Are there any existing design elements you want
included in the website design? Include logos,
company colours, bits from brochures or other design
elements you use.

_____

_____

_____

_____

4> What existing business designs do you want to keep?
These can be on your marketing material, your annual
report or on your existing website.

_____

_____

_____

_____

5> What designs do you want to make sure you get rid
of? These designs may be ones that were once
relevant but are no longer. The boss may have pointed
out a desire to get rid of some particular design
elements. Is there something about the current website
that simply must go?

_____

_____

_____

_____

What next?

Hiring the web providers to develop your website

Here are two conflicting statements:

> *'The days of web developers charging the world have gone.'*

> *'Paying peanuts gets you monkeys.'*

The fact is that both of these statements are true. Once upon a time it was the web guru (member of the mystic elite and your ticket to the Promised Land) who was in control. Many of these gurus were young designers who had learned how to code HTML. Some of them were businesspeople who saw the opportunity to ride the new economy wave and make big bucks in the process. (I've said enough on this topic.)

Many corporate websites cost their owners hundreds of thousands of dollars; some of them even cracked seven figures. Those days are more or less over. Unless you are a major corporate with some substantial integration planned, you shouldn't have to underwrite your whole business to finance your company website.

At the other end of the spectrum, the market is now full of small players churning out websites of all descriptions. Some of these are good; some of them are bad. As a rule, if you get your accountant's son (who has just discovered Microsoft FrontPage) to develop your corporate website, you are asking for trouble.

Believe it or not, the best websites are those designed and developed by experienced and skilled designers and web technicians. Many companies get their website built for under a thousand dollars. Most of them then spend twenty times that in time worrying about how they look online. 'It's only a temporary website. We got Frank's 16-year-old son to put it together. It's not bad for a first effort.' (It might be good for Frank's son, but is it good enough for your company?)

What to look for in a supplier

There are no hard and fast rules in selecting any supplier, but if it were up to me I'd look for the following:

Track record

They should have completed some company websites before yours. Don't be the guinea pig. Have a look at the style of what they have done and if the work looks sharp and up to par with what you see online, it's an excellent start.

Personal style

Like it or not, many designers have a personal style and set of preferences that tend to creep into most of the work they do. If a designer likes a particular genre of design, that genre is bound to echo throughout their work. Check their work and find the trends. If you like the stuff they are producing, great. If you really don't like something about their work, don't use them.

Process

Time to think like a businessperson. Deal with web designers who understand business. For starters they should provide you with a written proposal. The proposal should list the project in some detail, and give you costs for the work involved. It is OK for them to give you an estimate or cost range, especially if the brief is yet to be finalised and there are some issues that need to be resolved (as is usually the case).

The proposal should give you an indication of the time required to do the job, the payment terms, and any assumptions that have been made in the proposal that will affect the project and the price. If the proposal is a half-page document without an explanation of what is on offer, warning bells should be ringing (unless you are very flexible indeed).

The company should give you the definite impression that they have an understanding about what the job is all about.

Technical expertise

Unless you are planning to publish a very flat piece of static brochure-ware, it pays to see examples of work the company has done that require a bit of technological know-how. I prefer companies that are equipped to do both the design and technical development of the website. That way the chances that the two areas will work together are improved, and hence the project is likely to progress more smoothly. The sorts of things to look for include:

> Database feeds appearing on the websites

> The use of content management tools

> Basis utilities (such as email engines, secure areas, forms for completion by visitors) appearing on the websites

> Shopping cart and transaction capability.

Do you like them?

If they are not your cup of tea, find a provider that is. You are going to give them a major responsibility; also you may well need to spend quite of bit of time with them. Trust your instincts. All things considered, hire someone you trust and get along with.

When do you call them in?

Finish the Website Planner first. Understand what it is you are trying to achieve and in general terms how, before you add an extra voice to the crowd.

Do some research in conjunction with the Website Plan, over and above that required by the planning process itself. This way you will get a feel for how the Internet is being used today.

Discuss your website plan with others in your organisation. Depending on your role in the company, discuss it with your boss, the marketing manager, IT and the operations person. If you've established a strong rationale for your decisions the others will work with you to refine what you have done. (If you throw the issues up for discussion without having put in some definitive thought and recommendations, you might be trapped in the quagmire of committee-based decision-making.)

If there are strongly conflicting opinions within your business, thrash them out. Don't spend money developing the website and then waste time and money making large-scale changes later.

The most important thing this workbook will do is to give you a sound rationale for your website. The trick here is that the workbook will focus you on the important issues and needs that the website will meet. Web developers can drive your business website project. But why should they be the ones who determine how your business works and is portrayed to the world?

Let your business drive the solution, not the other way around.

Two years ago if you weren't selling your wares online your were missing the boat. I clearly remember bakers, shoe shops and fruit shops all clambering around to set up a shopping cart on their new websites. The truth is that if most of these businesses had a real think about their needs, they would have realised that they were wasting their time and money.

Getting a quote

The process of finding some preferred web providers should happen *before* you ask for formal proposals for the work involved. My advice is to identify two or three providers that feel right, according to the criteria I have mentioned, and then ask them for formal proposals (quotes).

If you go to market for proposals before working out whether you like the providers involved, you will end up making a decision that you won't be entirely satisfied with. It is likely that you will end up discounting some of the providers due to their poor track record, limited or irrelevant experience, limited resources, style, lack of methodology, and for other reasons I haven't thought of. You may find yourself stuck with by far the most expensive of the group or even without a viable option. Either way you may have to go through the whole exercise again, wasting time and money in the process.

I have provided an example 'Request for proposal' template at the end of the workbook for your reference. You will find it helpful if and when you go to market for proposals.

How much should you pay?

If you are a small businessperson on a shoestring budget, you should bank on spending at least $5,000. In case you are wondering, yes, I pulled this figure out of the air. This figure is at the low end of the spectrum. Having said that, there are very few single business websites that should cost over $200,000. The only way to get a feel for costs is to go to market and talk with others.

I'm not going to start giving my recommendations on costs here. I have no idea of your business needs and I would be wasting your time. There are a number of ways to find out what you should be paying for your website.

1> Complete this Planner and get three web providers that you have vetted to give a proposal. (Use the 'Request for proposal' template at the back of the Planner to help you.)

2> Talk with other companies that have websites that are similar to what you are after and ask them how much they paid. Whilst you are there, ask them who they used and whether they were happy with the service.

Don't be afraid to call people without an introduction. 'Hello [their name], I'm [your name] from [name of your business]. I am in the process of putting our website together. I understand you played a role in having your company website developed. Do you mind if I ask you a couple of questions about it?' If they say 'no' then there is no harm done. Chances are they will say something like 'Sure, what would you like to know?' At which point you are free to ask them what you want, and you will have made a new friend in the process.

Large versus small

If I ran a business turning over 50 million dollars a year I'd be looking to get the maximum out of the most important marketing and communications tool I have. (Again it depends on the business you are in and what you want to include on your website.)

Small web developers charge $40–$80 per hour for design work and $60–$150 for technical work. Larger companies may charge up to $250 per hour for their work. Personally I'm wary if the top end players charge top dollar for everything they do. For example, if I needed a company to help me re-key some content, I would not be happy if they tried to charge me at $250 per hour for 50 hours' clerical work. On the other hand, I can understand it if they charge me that sort of figure when they are developing complex content management and workflow applications.

The big companies should bring a sense of comfort to the table. They should have designers who have a strong track record and can walk the walk and talk the talk. They should be focused on your company achieving your business goals and less bent on getting back to the office so they can mock up a 'sample creative'. Watch out too for the big companies that have a history in everything technical except developing websites.

There are some advantages to using a larger more established web developer for your web project.

1> Because they have more resources, they are likely to be able to complete your project in a reasonable length of time.

2> They are likely to have more experience dealing with issues that may stop the small operator in their tracks.

3> If you are a larger organisation you are likely to have more than one project running concurrently. The larger provider will be able to help you with all of your web projects. (The more companies you have to work with, the more companies you have to work with.)

4> The more sophisticated providers are likely to bring a methodology to their project management. The more rigorous the attention to process and detail, particularly in the formative stages of planning, the less the chance of error and costly rework.

5> If something goes seriously wrong, you can sue them for damages to your business.

On the other hand, the smaller operators can be of value too.

1> The smaller guys have fewer infrastructures to support and are therefore often able to do things more cheaply.

2> If you can find a small operator who has really good skills and is very capable, you can adopt them as your personal supplier. To a big company you may be just another customer; to the small operator, you might be their number one client. Of course, this does not mean that you can push them around. If you make someone's life difficult, someone else will do the same for you. If a small provider bends over backwards to please you, reward them for it.

Sometimes it's worth paying more if you have a better chance of being happy with the job when it is done. It boils down to the size of your business and the degree to which prospects and customers will use the Internet to find out about your company.

Taking the project in-house

It is rare to find a person who has good design skills, is capable at database design and development, is proficient at web development, (Cold Fusion, ASP, Java) and the ability to work with management to address business issues and scope the ideal website solution for the company. Despite this, there are many companies who have placed individuals in charge of their website from the word 'go'.

Whilst the economic reasons for having a single person look after the website may make sense, it is rarely the best course of action for the majority of organisations.

The usual outcome is that concessions are made, usually with regard to graphic design and usability. If I had a dollar for every time I have heard staff groan about their website looking terrible because it was done in-house, I'd be able to afford one of those fat texts on Java programming.

The other problem that seems to arise is the project running well over time. Whilst I have no empirical evidence, I would suggest that this is because the person has underestimated the time it will take for them to complete the tasks with which they are less familiar. Whilst it is altruistic to allow your staff to learn new skills on the job, it can also be a painstaking and stop-start affair that no one appreciates. (Least of all the person being pressured to meet deadlines.)

Larger organisations get away with in-house development projects because they can justify having a complete web design and development team on the payroll.

From what I have seen, it usually pays to get an external web provider to design and develop your website. When the website has been delivered and bedded down, it makes sense to have an internal resource updating the website and its content as required. This person then has time on their side to improve their skills and assume the mantle of Webmaster.

Some thoughts on professionalism

Maybe this section should be titled 'Ways to look good and get ahead.' The following advice relates to the handling of your web providers. Respected 'professional' managers typically have the ability to get the best out of those around them. Be they colleagues, subordinates, superiors or business partners (read web providers), the professional managers treat them in such a manner that they are motivated to do their best, with and for the manager concerned.

Here are some ideas on treating your web provider well so they will be motivated to do their best for you.

> Having a definite vision for your website that relates to your business makes you more professional (hence this Planner).

> If you have not resolved all of the website issues and details, tell your web provider and work with them to find the right solution.

> When a decision is made regarding the website project, make sure your web provider receives a written copy. Documenting decisions and agreements to everyone in your organisation and leaving out the web provider is a sure way to end up being blamed for errors that occur (and rightly so).

> Document all aspects of the project so that all parties know exactly what is expected. Assume the web provider will do nothing more than what has been agreed and documented. (They cannot afford to deviate from what is written lest they expose themselves to risk.)

> When the requirements of the project change mid-stream, expect that the provider will have to charge for the changes. Invite them to provide a written quote for the extra work. Do not make them ask for the extra money, much less beg.

If you are in pickle because you have made an error in your planning, stand up and claim the error. If you have planned the project and made an error, it is likely others have seen your plans and contributed (albeit inadvertently) to that error. Even if you were not properly prepared, grab the error with both hands and claim it as yours. Then, working with your team and the web provider, come up with the required fix, take it to management, and move on. We all make mistakes. Learn from your mistakes. Try to cover them up or blame others at your peril. Saying that the web providers 'should have known' about something that is not documented is a waste of breath. If it was not documented, it is your fault!

Usually, when a person makes mistakes it means they are trying something. If management knows you are trying things that are feasible and in the best interests of the business, they will respect you for it. It may be the best performer who makes the most mistakes, because they are the ones contributing most to the business.

If there is one constant in business, it is that customers who are friendly, supportive, communicative, honest and good payers always get looked after. In the world of website development these are the people who also document all relevant details, issues and changes. They are also the ones who do their utmost to plan ahead, and give the web provider all of the information and support they can. They do not try to cut every dollar out of the contract and crunch the provider on price at every turn.

These same customers are the ones whose projects come in on time and on budget. Their providers also do that bit extra for them, to make sure the end product is as good as it can be. For some reason, these people end up being the 'good managers' mentioned before.

Tell your colleagues, managers, staff and your web provider that you have used the Website Planner as your guide to develop your website plan. Good managers make the most of resources that are available to them. No one is expected to know it all. Doctors read instructional journals, teachers use manuals, consultants 'cheat' on positively everything, and good managers choose carefully what they read and follow through with processes such as this workbook.

We only learn from what we put into action. No one text is the 'best thing' to read. Find one that looks right and devour it. Read it, learn it, and understand it.

By the way, nothing is more wasteful than managers who spend company dollars on all sorts of texts and journals, stack them neatly on their shelves, sometimes in multiple copies, and read none of them.

The process of website development

The following ideas relate to the process of developing your website with your chosen provider. Despite the fact that every project is different in size and context, here are some standard issues and milestones that you will have to address.

Getting the detail right

If you have worked through this workbook you will have gone a long way to being able to answer the questions the web provider is going to ask. For starters, show them the completed workbook, not just the brief you prepared for the 'Request for proposal' (RFP).

Unless you have pinned down all of the website functionality already, you and your web provider will need to agree on exactly how the final solution will function before any development begins. (Hopefully the providers have given you an idea of how they will approach this process as part of their initial proposal.) Take time to sort the issues out in detail, document them carefully and sign them off. Remember, unless there is a clear, unambiguous blueprint for the project, mistakes will be made (100% bulletproof certainty).

If errors are made and the correct solution has not been documented, then you do not have grounds to complain. (Things that are said in meetings a week before the project commenced mean nothing.) You must document all details and their amendments into a single specification of the job that is signed off by all parties. (When I say single I am referring to a single version. Copies can be made, but foolish is the person who allows copies of superseded versions to remain in circulation.)

Contract review

Despite the best intentions of all parties, there may come a time when 'even the best laid plans' have to change. This process cannot be taken lightly.

> Face it, if your builder has started building a house with three bedrooms, and half way through you decide you need four bedrooms instead, it is going to take the builder some time to redraw the plans, undo some of the work he has already completed, and start again with a different result in mind. This all costs money and you will have to pay it.

Depending on what sorts of changes you come up with during the development project, you may be required to finance the change in direction. Sometimes seemingly simple changes in tack can mean fundamental shifts in approach.

When a change occurs, large or small, you owe it to yourselves and your provider to amend the website specifications and the contract where applicable. A customer who keeps moving the goalposts, albeit fractionally, will soon waste everybody's time and patience. Unless the customer is prepared to pay for the changes they demand, they will quickly erode the constructive relationship that exists between them and their provider.

The creative rounds

The term 'creative rounds' refers to the iterative process whereby the web designer takes a brief from you and comes back with their designs.

Note: The web designer is the person with graphical design skills who specialises in website design.

First up, the designer will be looking for themes to underpin the graphic design (look and feel) of the website. The initial input you might provide includes:

> Existing and established company designs (logos, colours, posters, and preferred artwork) and any established design rules that surround them.

> Information on how you want your business to be perceived. Style, size, progressiveness, environmental approach, friendliness and so on. This is the stuff that goes into developing the company brand.

> Examples of websites that you like and some that you don't like and explanations of why.

> If you have an annual report that you like, that will be worth including.

The designer will try to gather as much information as they can to develop an understanding of what you require.

The challenge for the designer is to go away and come up with one or two designs that they believe best represents what they have learned about your company.

> Asking for five designs to choose from up front defeats the purpose. The designer will be looking for a 'best fit' not five reasonable fits. Also, it serves little purpose if you choose different parts of five different designs and ask the designer to piece them together. Chances are the three, four or five elements will have no relationship to each other and look lousy when grouped on the page or screen.

Focus on establishing the single most appealing design first. Derivative designs for associated websites and other media such as PowerPoint presentations can be created later.

Now, this is where the creative rounds come in. Your job is to methodically examine what the designer has given you (as a first round). You need to establish what you like and what you don't like about the design provided. Take time to discuss what the design is about, before shooting it to pieces. Sometimes there are specific rationales for design elements that are well worth discussing. Having said that, if you really decide that what they have provided is way off the mark, don't let them believe otherwise.

The feedback that you provide is critical. Where you say you like something, the designer will take that element and 'lock it in'.

> Do not give the designer hurried feedback now on the basis that you can change it later. (You can, but at what cost?)

> Do work methodically through all of the design elements and select those that are to stay and those that are to go.

> Do get the input of at least one other 'qualified' person within your company. If appropriate, get hold of your senior managers and discuss in detail the designs presented. (Have the designer present so they can get a first hand reading from the feedback provided.)

> Do not 'sit' on the design for a week. You will be slowing down the entire process and you will find you have forgotten much of what you and the designer have discussed at earlier meetings. Get the feedback to the designer ASAP!

> Be prepared to 'sign off' on the annotations and feedback that you have given to the designer. (Yes, your head is on the block.)

The designer will take your comments and input away and revise the original designs in line with what has been said and written. Soon, they will be back with Round 2 for you and your team to review. The process now repeats itself.

Consider this: If a project has been quoted on the basis of three creative rounds, this is your last chance to make things right. The designer will take this second round of feedback and incorporate it into a new design. What they provide in return is in fact the third round of creative input. You can of course continue to alter the design of the website whenever you want, just make sure you have your chequebook with you when you do.

Some designers are more flexible than others are when it comes to the process of creative rounds. My advice is to treat them with the same commitment you give to the three-round designers. The longer the creative process is drawn out, the more chances there are for confusion, disappointment and error. Throw all of your energies at resolving the design with your team and the designer and the project will benefit from it. (If you set a precedent of quick and effective decision-making, the designer will be more inclined to cut you some slack later on if it is required.)

One more thing. The best way to view any design element of a web project is online. See if you can get your web provider to put the creative rounds, especially numbers two and three, on a test-server for you to access and review by web browser over the Internet. This way you will be able to see how the designs actually appear online where they will ultimately be used. Not all providers have the facility to do this, but the bigger guys certainly should. Looking at printouts of the website may not give an accurate representation of colour, layout, size and texture.

When the provider displays these designs online, don't expect them to function like the completed website. They are for visual verification only.

Manage that website

When all is said and done, and the website is up and running, it needs to be managed. The best way to achieve this is by setting some Key Performance Indicators (KPIs) by which you will 'point score' the success of your website.

Refer to the original objectives of the website for your KPIs. Depending on what your objectives were, you should be able to give a score out of ten for each criterion. I'd suggest you put a note in your diary to review the website's performance on a quarterly basis. This will give you a prompt to review trends, including:

> traffic flow patterns

> content updates

> feedback

> sources of sales inquiries

> effect of phone calls

> costs of distributing marketing and technical materials

> changes in existing processes

Analyse the results and make recommendations or decisions accordingly. The website is there to be improved. If you can identify ways to continue improving your business through your website, you will continue to open new doors for yourself and your business.

How are you going to measure the success of the website? List five measures that you are going to put in place.

_____

_____

_____

_____

_____

13

Request for proposal (RFP) template

The following is a suggested format for the document you give to potential web providers. The content is highly generic and I would encourage you to be thinking about your business when you use it. If it needs to be changed then by all means go ahead.

Introduction

Purpose

This RFP is designed to provide interested web professionals with the information required to make a proposal to [your company] for the design and development of the new website at [your company's website address].

Due date

Submissions will be accepted up until [nominate a time and date at a minimum 10 working days from the date they receive the RFP].

Contact

For any assistance relating to this RFP and the project involved, please contact [person's name and contact details including phone and email address].

Section 1 — Project brief

Company background

General information on company.

Refer to other sources of information about the company such as the existing website, brochures, or the current annual report which is available from [contact person's name].

Mention any current news or activities that are significant and/or have a bearing on the current project.

Website objectives

Refer to the objectives you listed in the Website Planner. (This will help the providers focus their thinking.)

Target audiences

Refer to the target audiences you listed in this Website Planner. (The providers need to understand the audiences if you want them to give you suggestions on how they might approach the project.)

Website content

Refer to all of the content items you listed in this Website Planner.

You need to list information about everything that's going to appear on your website. I'd suggest doing it in a tabular format like the one following:

Content overview

Name	Type	Pages required	Update process	Comment
Company history	Text and pics	1 page	Static content	Fixed text with 2 photos of old products
Product catalogue	Text and photos	Query page, display page	Database driven	SQL database of product information and images to feed website
Case studies	Text and pics	1 per case study	Content management application (CMA)	John will add case studies when they occur using a simple template-driven CMA. New case study expected weekly. Need ability to add, delete, amend and archive. No approval process required.
Feedback	Email form	1 form	Not required	Simple email form for people to send their comments regarding the website

Explain all of the terms you use that might be misinterpreted. Write down clearly what you mean by terms like: Content Management Application (CMA), database-driven, template-driven, forms, workflow, approval and so on.

Make sure the whole of your website has been described in the table. The providers will then be able to understand exactly what they are quoting on.

Project timing

Give the providers a good idea of your required and anticipated timing for the project. Include:

> Due date of proposals

> Selection of successful provider and notification to all

> Project commencement

> Due date for any part or all of the website. (Advise the providers if this date is flexible. Again, make sure this date is realistic or there will be issues.)

Proposal format

How do you want to receive the proposals?

> Hard copy

> Multiple hard copy

> Original and copies that are marked 'Original' and 'Copies'

> Softcopy (for example, PDF or Word)

> **A Word of Advice**

Do not ask all of the providers to submit multiple copies of extensive proposals unless you really need them to make your assessment. Are the people for whom you are making copies really going to want to read them? Nothing is worse than spending hours generating multiple copies of long complex submissions, and seeing them sitting unread on the floor outside the office of the project coordinator in question. (They are easy to spot. Firstly, there is often a huge pile of them depending on how many companies submitted proposals and how many copies were required, and secondly, your eyes are drawn immediately to the very familiar binding and covers that you spent hours sweating over.) Think of the environment too; how much paper and other consumables are you wasting?

The decision-making process

If there are any unusual processes that have to occur, let the providers know up front. Some examples include:

> People who need to be consulted interstate.

> If the primary contact is unavailable for some time before the proposal due date, give the name and contact details of a secondary contact.

> Anticipated delays in decision-making processes.

> Legal processes that need to be considered due to the nature of your business.

> Any processes of certification or qualification the providers must comply with that will affect their consideration. (Government tenders sometimes stipulate that tendering companies are registered on a 'preferred supplier' register before tendering. The process of becoming a 'preferred supplier' might be quite a task in itself.)

Existing marketing material

You should not ask the providers to provide any creative input at this stage (it just serves to clutter the decision-making process). Despite this, it is a good idea to let the providers know what material is available for them to develop the look and feel of the website. If you can, attach some examples of brochures of other designs that you are happy with. Tell the providers if your annual report is worth looking at too, particularly if it is online. The more you can demonstrate that you are prepared to support the successful provider with the job, the more confident they will be in giving you a competitive quote for the project. (On the other hand, if they suspect you have no idea and that they will have to do all of the work, they are going to have to build in a big cash buffer to make sure they don't lose money on the project.)

The budget

Don't think that you are being clever by not telling the providers how much you have to spend. The facts are:

> If your budget is tight and your scope broad, the chances are the providers will quote above what you have to spend, and you will have wasted everyone's time.

> If you have a generous budget for your website, the providers will quote on what they believe is the best solution for you. You can still compare what they have given you and choose the lowest price.

> If you tell them you have $20,000 to spend when you have $50,000, the providers will give you a price for the most economically suitable solution. You will be left wondering about the functionality that you have forfeited, and end up asking for additional information under the guise of 'newly available funds'. Again, you will have wasted everyone's time.

> If the budget is totally unrealistic, the providers will come and tell you so. That will give you the opportunity to re-think what you will include in the current phase of the project, and what you will defer to later.

A sample site map

Despite the fact that you will be looking to the web provider to assist you in the creation of the site architecture, it is not a bad idea to provide what you think might be the best architecture to begin with.

> You might have the best solution and if so you will give the providers a clearer picture of the project.

> You may well be right off the track, in which case the providers will come to the initial stages of the project prepared to assist you with this facet of the website.

> By understanding the website architecture and its rationale, you will be more in control of the project in general.

Technologies

If you have a good reason for wanting the website to be built using particular software, then you must say so in the RFP. Here are some example reasons:

> The website is to be maintained in-house using particular software. You want it to be developed in that same software, or in a manner that will facilitate your in-house maintenance.

> Your internal databases are a certain type and you want the website to use those databases so you don't have to spend time and money setting up alternative databases. Examples of the databases include MS SQL, MS Access, Oracle and Sybase.

> The website is to be hosted by a specific ISP and they only support certain software.

> You have determined that you do not want to pay an additional fee to the ISP for supporting particular software. (For example, many providers charge an additional fee for supporting Cold Fusion. They charge the fee to offset the moneys they pay to maintain a Cold Fusion licence.)

Hosting

Your RFP can include the set up and management of the website hosting or that can be tackled later with your selected provider. Either way, you need to give the providers whatever information you have relating to the hosting of the website. Some examples include:

> The name of your ISP if have decided to go with a specific one.

> Rough details of an existing ISP contract you have and whether or not you mind changing ISPs when the contract is over.

> The database and website building technologies you require.

> The expected number of user sessions that will occur per week (roughly).

> The availability required of the website. (If you were planning to advertise to local businesses, I would not worry too much about 24x7 availability of the website. The key will be that the website is available from, say, seven in the morning to ten at night. The more latitude the ISP is given to have the system disconnected for maintenance reasons, the cheaper the hosting costs.)

> Do you need a dedicated web server? Do you want the ISP to host your website on its own computer? You might if you are expecting thousands of people to access your website on a daily basis. If this is the case, you should be speaking with the larger ISPs, or 'hosting providers' (as they call themselves) direct. If you are a small- to medium-sized business that expects a few dozen user sessions on a good day, this is not an issue you need to consider. Besides, the costs of having a dedicated computer to host your website are considerable.

Ongoing website management

> Do you want the web provider to manage all changes and updates to your website?

> Do you want them to meet with you on a regular basis to discuss changes in content and presentation?

> Do you want to be able to update your own content but to get the provider to make design changes?

> Do you want to be able to cover all options by getting the providers to give you pricing for each scenario?

Think about the best solution for you and include it in your brief. If you plan regular content updates to the website and commit to them in advance with your provider, you will get a better price for them than if you call the provider on an ad hoc basis.

Selection criteria

It is a good idea to provide a list of the criteria by which you will be selecting the successful web provider. This will ensure the providers focus on responding to the important areas as you see them. Refer to the following example:

Criteria	Weighting (1 to 5)
Relevant experience	4
Resources available	3
Project methodology	3
Understanding of issues	4
Project timing	2
Price	3
Design expertise	4
Database expertise	5

Terms of RFP

Although the likelihood of argument about an RFP is remote, it is a good idea to spell out a few terms relating to this process, such as:

> Costs incurred in the preparation and delivery of responses are not refunded.

> All responses to this RFP will be treated in confidence.

> [Your organisation] reserves the right to accept or reject any proposal.

> [Your organisation] is not bound to accept the lowest price.

> [Your organisation] cannot be held responsible for any damages incurred as a result of this RFP.

> [Your organisation] reserves the right to reject all proposals submitted.

This is not a comprehensive list by any means; and is not a recommendation as to the legal position of your RFP. If you are concerned about your position with regard to the process of requesting proposals, you should seek your own legal advice.

Section 2—Information required

The following is what you should ask for from the responding providers:

Company details

Name

Ownership

Location(s)

Number of staff

Experience

Portfolio of work

Examples of relevant projects

Referees (I suggest you ask for two referees)

Account/Project management team

Who will look after your project? (Not all projects require a large team to manage them.) Ask for a brief summary of each person's relevant skills and experience.

Account manager

Project manager

Chief designer

Chief technical person

You may receive submissions for syndicates of people who are working together. For example a designer may team up with a technical person and together bid for projects. I have no problems with this if the group concerned can demonstrate that they are able to work together. (Ask them what jobs they have done as individuals and together as a team.)

Project approach and timelines

By asking how the providers plan to tackle your website project, you will get an idea of how they work. They are likely to provide a range of details, which may include their project methodology, milestones and timelines, the facets of your project that they believe require careful consideration. This will provide an insight into their experience and sophistication.

> A web provider with real-world experience managing projects should be able to put this question into perspective. By their nature, website development projects have a number of generic steps or processes that need to occur for the project to be successful. The web providers should be able to identify some project milestones and give you an estimated timeline. If they can't answer this question, how did they work out the figures they have quoted?

Interactive elements

For each of the interactive elements of the website (and you should list them in the RFQ) you should ask how the provider plans to provide the solution. You should include all elements that are not static web pages. For example:

> Email forms

> Surveys

> Virtual tours

> Shopping carts

> Rollovers (icons or elements that change when the user rolls their cursor over the top of them)

> Multimedia elements (such as sound and video)

> Games or interactive quizzes

> Content management applications

> Store locator

> Forums and chat rooms

> Secure areas

Pricing

The submission should clearly spell out what the pricing includes and provide either a firm cost or a limited range of costs for the project. Sometimes it is not feasible for the providers to quote a firm figure for the work because the client (you) has not provided sufficient information. (How long is a piece of string?) By completing this RFP template you will go a long way to providing the detail required.

As far as the range of pricing is concerned, the provider should indicate which part of the project is unclear and requires the range. You as the client will have to provide the required information if you want a firm price. The providers should ultimately be in a position to recommend a solution and provide you with a price for that solution.

Ongoing work

My recommendation is to get the providers to give you a figure for ongoing changes to the website, even if this is not part of your plan. Give yourself the flexibility to call upon the provider at times of need.

> Price per hour for design work

> Price per hour for technical work

> Price for a monthly or bi-monthly half-day commitment to you

> Minimum fee for any work

If you are going to get the web provider to do all of your content updates, then it is a good idea to book a regular (perhaps monthly) slab of time. This will ensure that you get your updates even when times are busy. At least the provider will then give you relative priority over a long queue of pending jobs.

The web provider may well offer to provide you with a quote or proposal when ad hoc jobs come up. This is perfectly fine, as you cannot expect them to quote on a project without a brief.

Other relevant input

My recommendation is to ask the web providers to submit any other information that they feel is relevant to the project and the selection process. They may provide:

> Suggestions for your project. (Yours to keep, even if you do not use their services.)

> Examples of other projects they have done, which make them attractive as a provider. (The provider may have specific systems, design or project experience that parallels the needs of your organisation.)

> Examples of projects they have done where you know the people involved. (Good source of reference information.)

> Information which demonstrates an understanding of certain issues that face your organisation, which make them a good choice.

Index